ONE SKY ABOVE US

The Story of Chief Joseph and the Nez Perce Indians

NANCY PLAIN

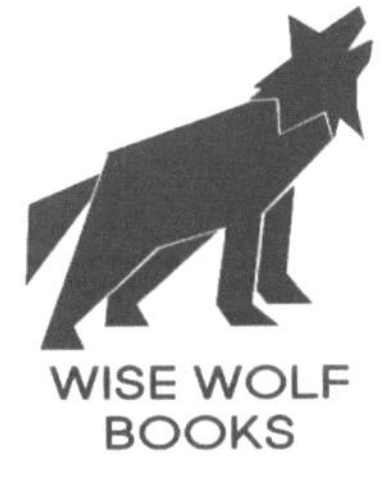

ALSO BY NANCY PLAIN

Go West, George Catlin

Sagebrush and Paintbrush

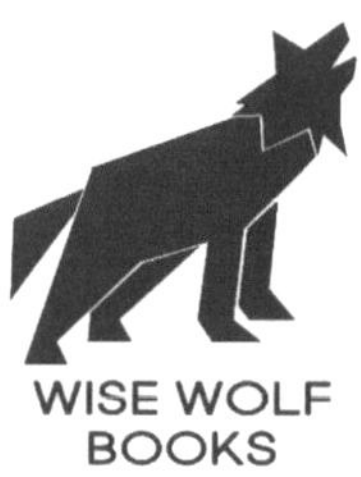

WISE WOLF BOOKS
An Imprint of Wolfpack Publishing
wisewolfbooks.com
9850 S. Maryland Parkway, Suite A-5 #323, Las Vegas, Nevada 89183

Paperback ISBN 978-1-953944-96-2
eBook ISBN 978-1-953944-95-5

ONE SKY ABOVE US

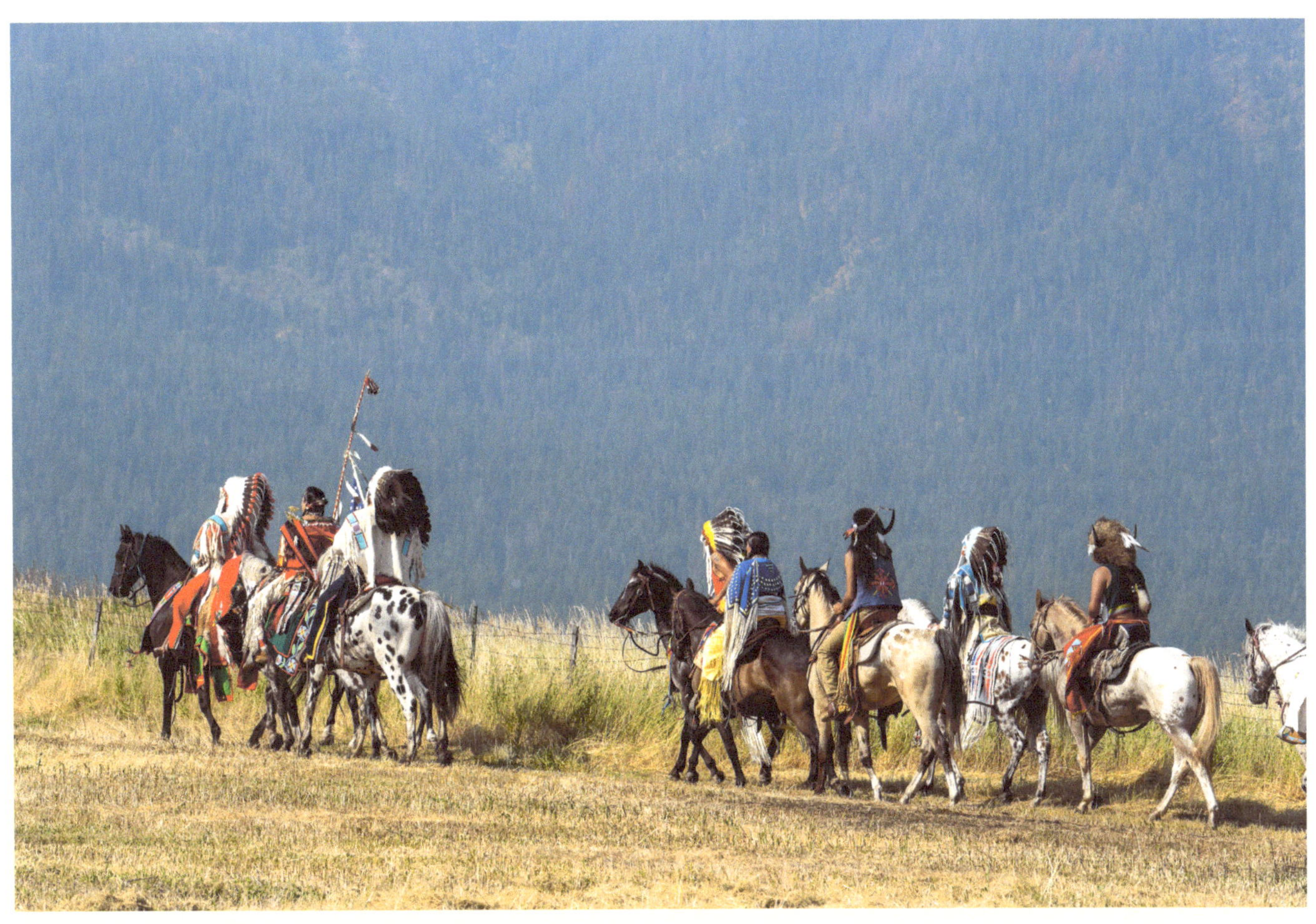

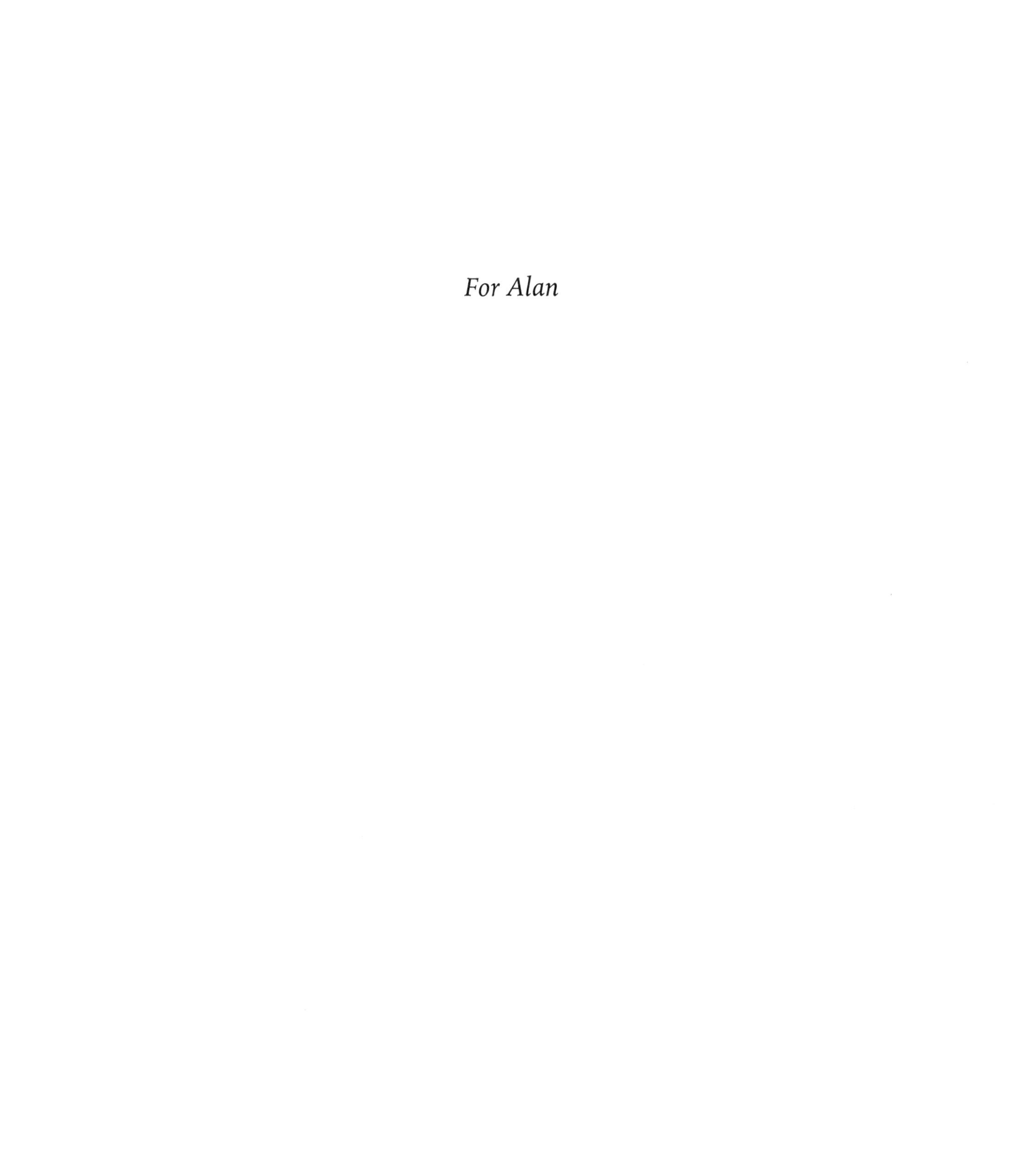

For Alan

Introduction

I Belong to the Land

IT WAS SUMMERTIME in the green Wallowa Valley. In his camp by the shining river, Old Chief Joseph lay dying. His last thoughts were of the things he loved most—his people and the land. For a long time, white people—the American settlers—had been eyeing his country. Now, in this very year, 1871, they had come into the valley for the first time. Joseph knew that many more would follow. He took his son's hand and said, "My son, my body is returning to my Mother Earth, and my spirit is going very soon to see the Great Spirit Chief... Always remember that your father never sold his country. You must stop your ears whenever you are asked to sign a treaty selling your home... My son, never forget my dying words. This country holds your father's body. Never sell the bones of your father and your mother."

Old Chief Joseph and his family were Nez Perce Indians. Nez Perce is French for "pierced nose." The name was given to the tribe in earlier days when some of its members had

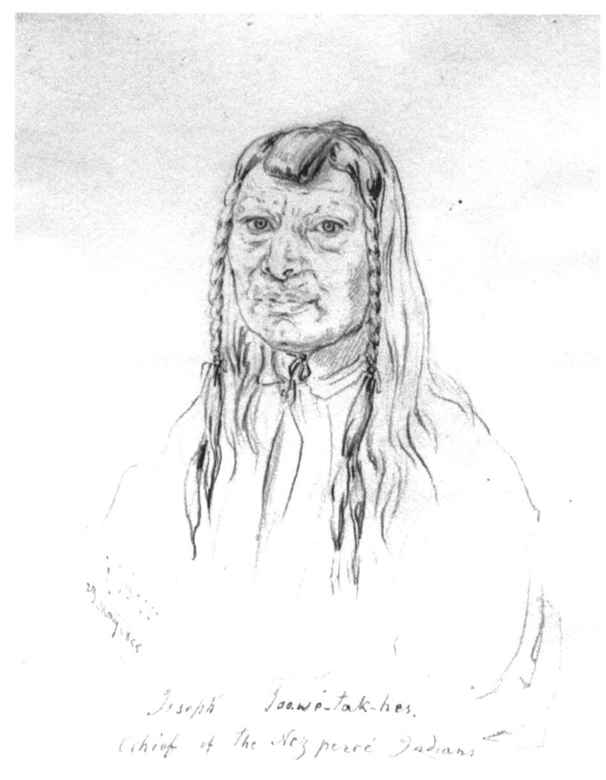

This drawing of Old Chief Joseph, also known as Joseph the Elder, was created on May 29, 1855, by Gustav Soon. Gustav was an Indian interpreter for the U.S. Arm with a talent for drawing and painting.

decorated their noses with pieces of seashell. But the Indians had their own name for their tribe. They called themselves the Nee-me-poo, which in their language means "the People."

The People were proud and free. They had lived in the American Northwest long before there was a country called America. For thousands of years, their home was the place where parts of three states now meet—Idaho, Oregon, and Washington.

Their land was wild and beautiful. It was guarded by snow-topped

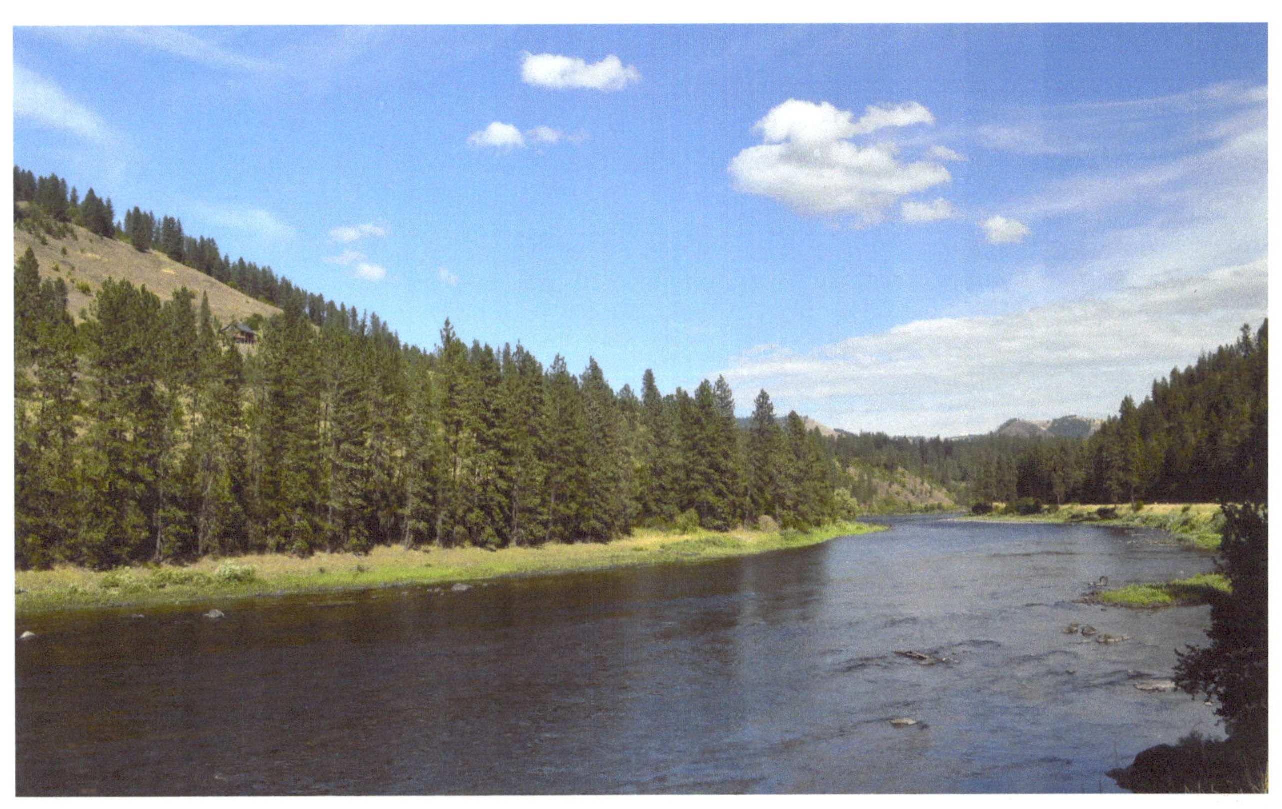

The Clearwater River cuts through the New Perce reservation.

mountains, from the Bitterroots in the east to the Blue Mountains in the west. It was crossed by rushing rivers. The Clearwater, the Salmon, the Imnaha, and the Grande Ronde rivers all flowed into the mighty Snake. The waters of Nez Perce country created fertile valleys and cut deep canyons into the land. Hell's Canyon of the Snake River is the deepest gorge in all of North America.

The land meant life to the People. Rivers and creeks gave them fish. From the rich earth, the Indians collected good things to eat. They hunted for game in the hills and dark forests. And they moved with the changing seasons, as animals migrated and fruits ripened. They took shelter from winter snow in the canyon bottoms. In the high country, they escaped the summer heat. It was as one great warrior said, "The earth is part of my body. I belong to the land out of which I came. The earth is my mother."

Above all, the Nez Perce were horse people. They were fearless riders, as easy on horseback as they were on their own feet. Miles of grassy prairie in their homeland provided food for huge herds. The People were famous for their breeding skill. They raised strong, swift animals. Some of these were the spotted type called Appaloosa. Horses gave the Indians freedom—freedom to travel far, to ride like the wind.

The tribe was divided into separate bands. Each had its own territory and was governed by its own chief and council of elders. Old Chief Joseph's band was the largest one. It was in the Wallowa country of northeastern Oregon. The Wallowa, protected by mountains and canyons, was hard to reach. So Joseph's people were among the last of their tribe to be affected by the great wave of whites who were settling the West.

It had started slowly, with a few explorers and fur traders in the early 1800s. Then came gold miners and pioneers—more every year on the Oregon Trail. As the newcomers became farmers and ranchers, they often settled on Indian land. By the time Old Chief Joseph died, many tribes in the West had already been forced onto reservations.

After hearing Old Chief Joseph's last words, his son remembered, "I pressed my father's hand and told him I would protect his grave with my life. My father smiled and passed away to the spirit land.

"I buried him in that beautiful valley of winding waters. I love that land more than all the rest of the world."

This son, called "Young Joseph" by the whites, was then named chief of the Wallowa band. He was 31 years old. In just a few years, America would come to know him as the famous Chief Joseph, leader of his people.

Chapter One

Faithful Friends

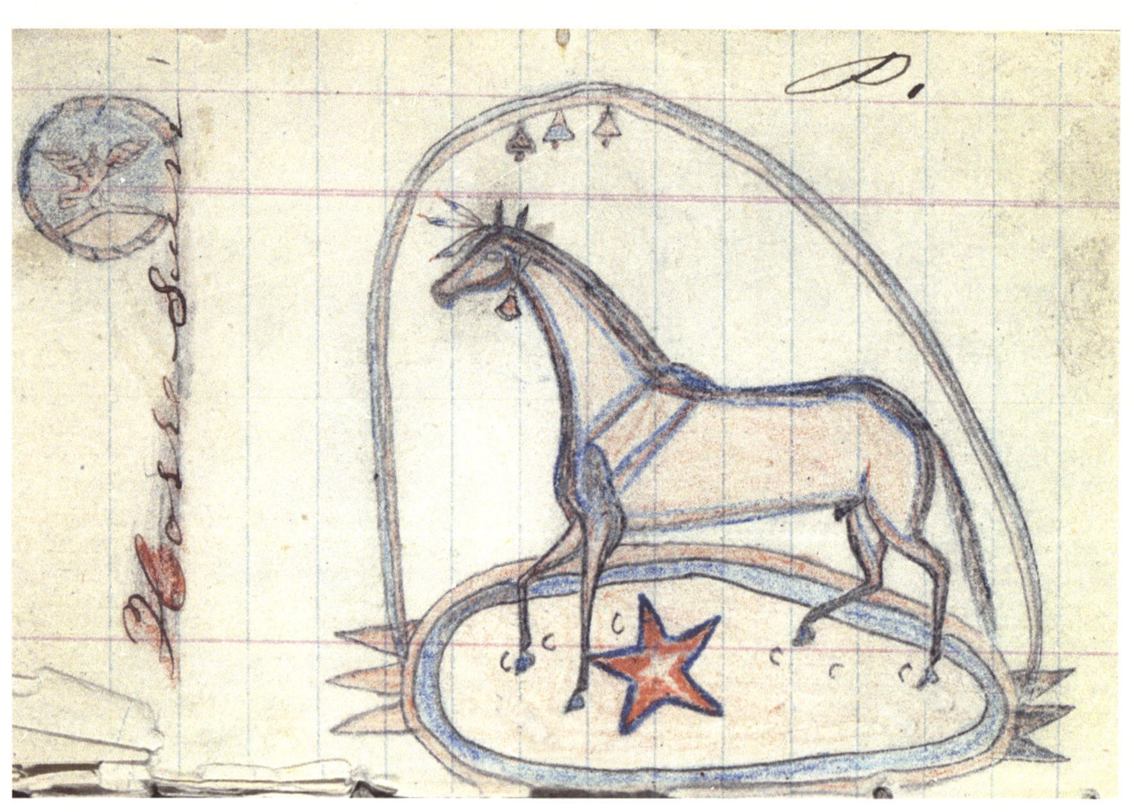

OLD CHIEF JOSEPH was young when the first white men came to Nez Perce country. His band lived too far away to meet them, but he heard the news and wondered about the strangers, who seemed to come from another world. They were the explorers of the Lewis and Clark Expedition. They had been sent by President Thomas Jefferson and were the first U.S. citizens ever to cross the continent all the way to the Pacific Ocean. After struggling over the Rocky Mountains, Captain Meriwether Lewis and Captain William Clark had hoped to find an easy all-water route to the sea. Instead, they had to cross the dreaded Bitterroot Mountains—"the most terrible mountains I ever beheld," wrote one member of the party. On the steep Lolo Trail, the men were freezing and so near starving that they killed and ate one of their horses.

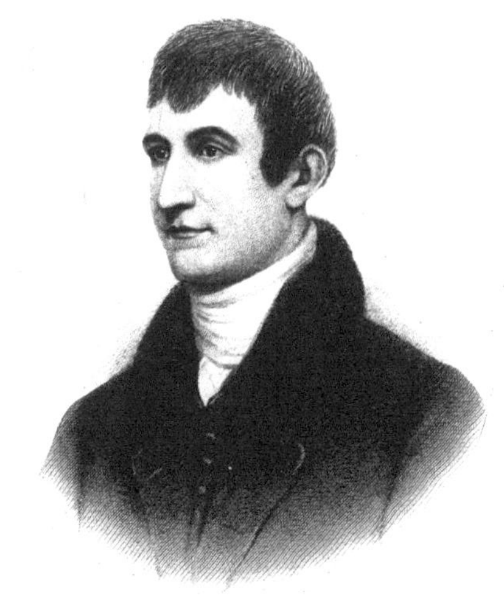

Captain Merriwether Lewis

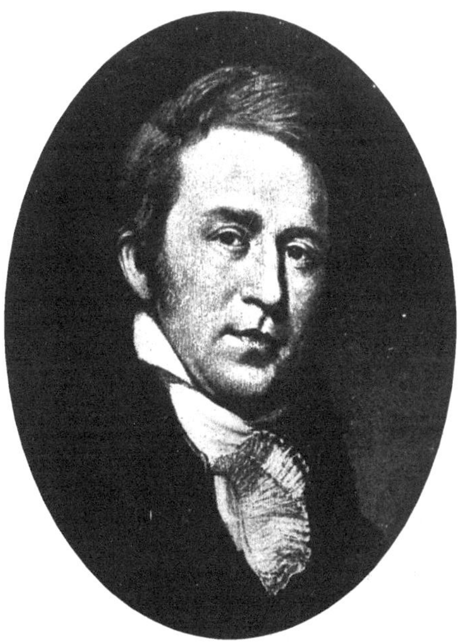

Captain William Clark

On September 20, 1805, they came

down from the Bitterroots onto a place called Weippe Prairie. These ragged, pale-skinned travelers startled a band of Nez Perce who were camped nearby. But the Indians, led by Chief Twisted Hair, welcomed the explorers and gave them food. Without Nez Perce help, the men might never have reached the Pacific Ocean. Twisted Hair pointed the way on an elk-hide map. He let the Americans cut down trees to make canoes. He and another chief even guided the men hundreds of miles downstream to the Columbia—the great river that would bring the Expedition to the sea.

In the spring of 1806, on their way home, Lewis and Clark returned to Nez Perce country. The captains asked the Indians to make peace with their enemies. With peace among all the tribes, the Americans could safely build fur-trading posts throughout the Northwest. The Nez Perces agreed to this; they were eager for white men's goods.

The captains thought the Nez Perce were the friendliest, most honorable Indians they had met on their long adventure. Captain Clark called

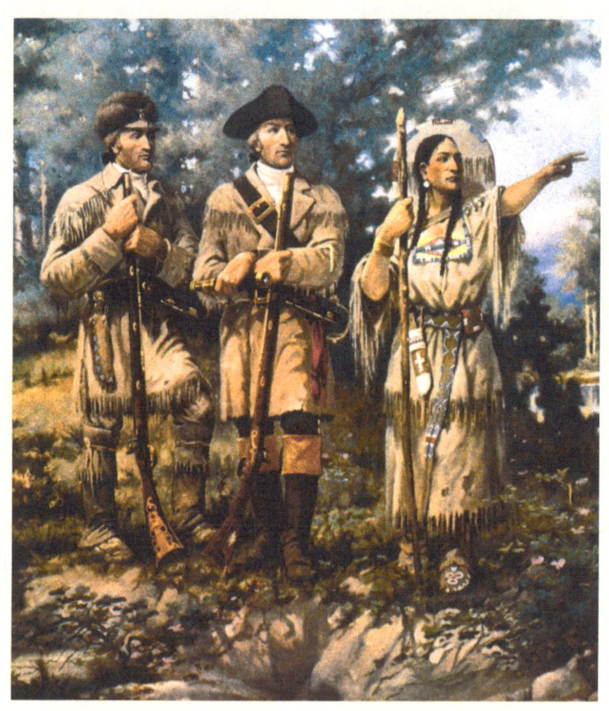

Using sign language and Indian interpreters, the two groups managed to talk to each other.

his two river guides his "faithful friends." Members of the tribe would also guide the Expedition back over the Bitterroots. Before the explorers left, whites and Indians exchanged presents. Toward the whites, "their hearts were good," the Nez Perce said. And they made a vow: They would be friends of the white men forever.

Still Nez Perce life followed its age-old pattern. Each band, in its own place, lived much the same as the others. To Old Chief Joseph's Wallowa band, their country was the most beautiful of all.

The Wallowas spent winter where it was warmest—in the canyon bottoms carved by running rivers. In these low valleys, the People lived in longhouses, with walls of bark and woven grass. Fire pits ran down the center of each house. There was room inside for many families. Winter was a time for storytelling, a time for grandparents to teach children the ways of the tribe. Women made baskets and clothes and prepared meals. Men repaired weapons, trained horses, and hunted for meat. The horses stayed in the canyon bottoms, too, with plenty of bunchgrass to eat.

In spring, when wildflowers colored the prairie, the band moved to higher ground. There the families lived in tepees, which the women moved

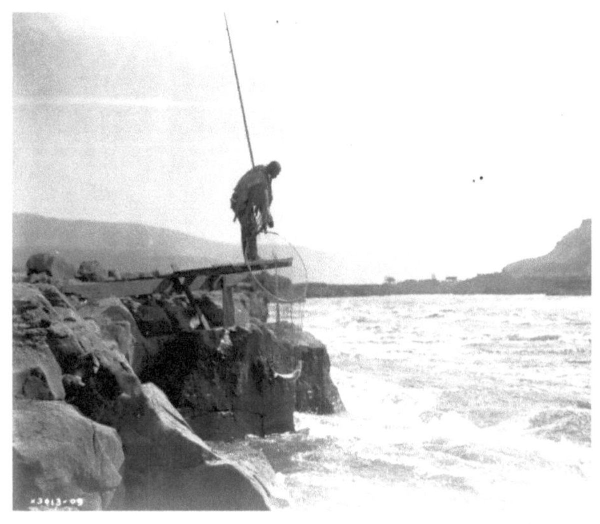

The Indians used spears and nets to catch the year's first salmon.

easily from one place to another. Spring was the time to start gathering vegetables to eat, such as carrots and wild potatoes and a root called kouse. Fishing season began then, too, as salmon were swimming upstream to lay their eggs. This tasty fish was the tribe's basic food.

In the heat of summer, the People moved up and up, to the cool, high Wallowa Valley itself. It was a magical place of snowy mountains, emerald meadows, and a deep, blue lake. The sparkling Wallowa River was now full of salmon. The Indians ate the fish fresh or else dried it for later use. Women and girls gathered juicy berries on the mountainside. In the meadows they dug with special sticks for the camas bulb. Baked in pits lined with hot stones, the bulb tasted sweet. Camas was eaten freshly cooked or pressed into cakes for hungry times in the future. Along with salmon it was the most important part of the Nez Perce diet.

Summertime was visiting time, too. The Wallowas liked to gather camas with other Nez Perce bands at Weippe Prairie. Digging was more fun for the women then, as they talked with relatives and friends. Men raced their best horses, hunted and fished, and played a gambling game with sticks. Band chiefs held councils. And at night there was dancing and singing and flirting among the young.

In the fall animals left the high valleys for lower ground. The Nez Perce bands followed them. The Wallowas had a favorite place where they hunted for elk, deer, antelope, rabbits, bears, and more. Then as the year rolled around to winter again, it was back to the village in the canyon.

The People's lives could not be separated from the world around them. They gave thanks to the animals and plants that they used in order to live. They believed that everything in nature had its own spirit, whether it was an ant, a bear, or a drop of rain. And spirits often gave their special powers to a person. These powers became that person's spirit helper, or *wyakin*—a protector for life.

When boys and girls were about lo to 13 years old, they went alone into

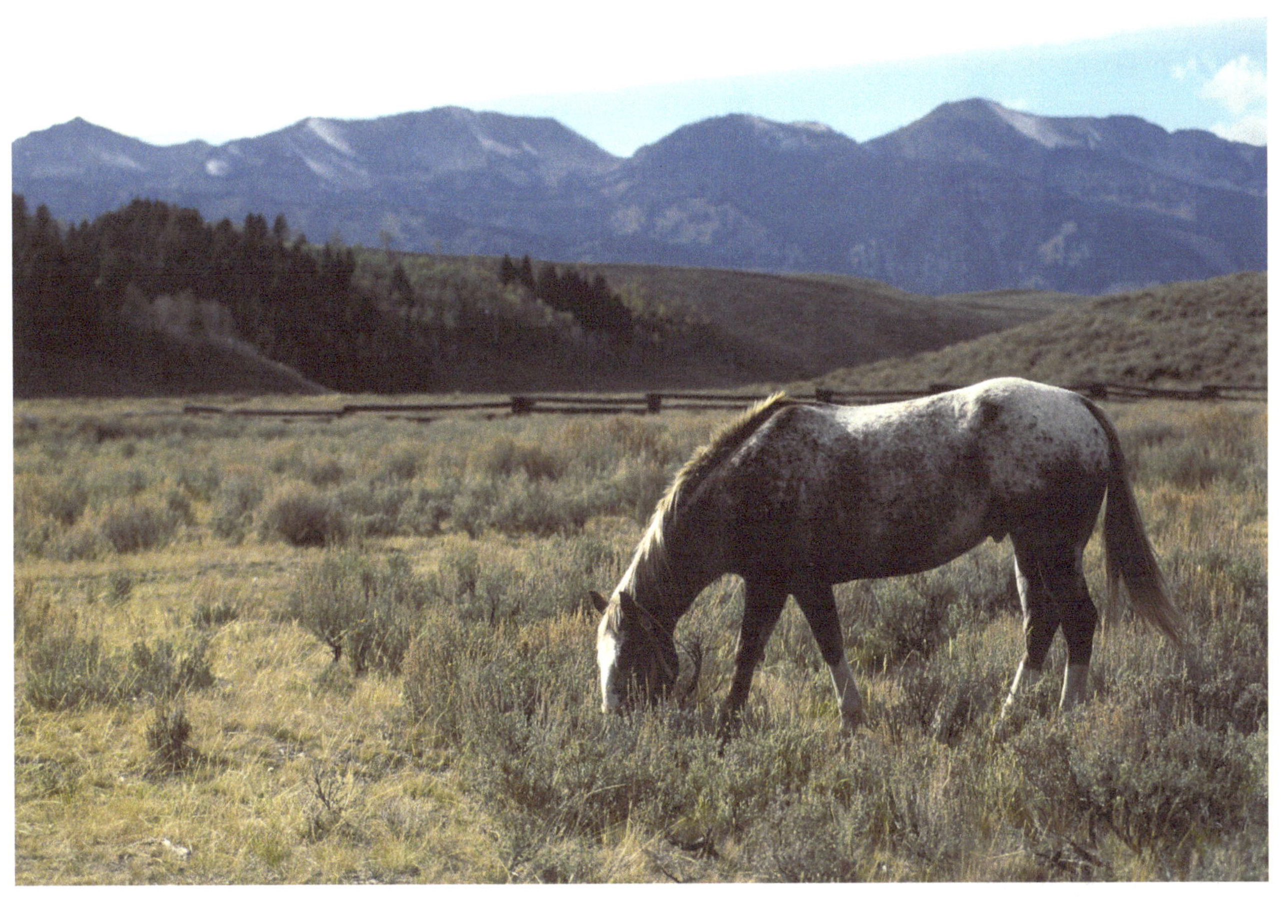

Appaloosa horse grazing on ranch in Sawtooth Valley Idaho by William Mullins.

the wilderness to seek their wyakin. It might come to them in real life or in a dream. It would always be kept a secret. The thunder spirit made a person brave. The deer wyakin gave the gift of speed. People called on their wyakin in times of need. They sang the song it had taught them. In this way each Nez Perce had a close link to the spirit world—and so to all of nature.

Another part of Nez Perce tradition came to be called the "Dreamer" faith. Dreamers worshipped the earth as their mother. They believed that the land was a gift from the Creator, theirs to live on forever. The earth should never be bought or sold, planted or plowed, or changed in any way, the Dreamers said. Even cutting the grass was wrong. "...do I dare cut off my mother's hair?" a Dreamer prophet asked.

The Nez Perce homeland was in a larger part of the Northwest called the Columbia Plateau. There were many tribes in this region—Cayuse, Palouse, Walla Walla, Umatilla, Yakima, Spokan, and others. Most of these had much in common with each other. But the Nez Perce tribe was the largest and most powerful of all.

The Nez Perce loved to travel and trade. Their fine horses, their main source of wealth, were in demand throughout the West. Other products they traded were furs, dried foods, and their famed bows, made from the horns of mountain sheep. When the People traveled west toward the Pacific Ocean, they exchanged these goods for things like seashells and shellfish. When they rode east, they left the Columbia Plateau, crossed the mountains, and entered the Great Plains. There they traded and hunted, racing bareback across the prairie after the thundering buffalo herds.

From the Plains tribes, the Nez Perce learned to make tepees and to wear long, eagle-feather war bonnets.

The Lewis and Clark Expedition did open the way for more trading posts in the Northwest. The Nez Perce acquired many things from the whites, such as tobacco, woolen clothes, beads, and blankets. But the biggest prize was guns. With guns, Nez Perce hunters could defend themselves in buffalo country against their enemies,

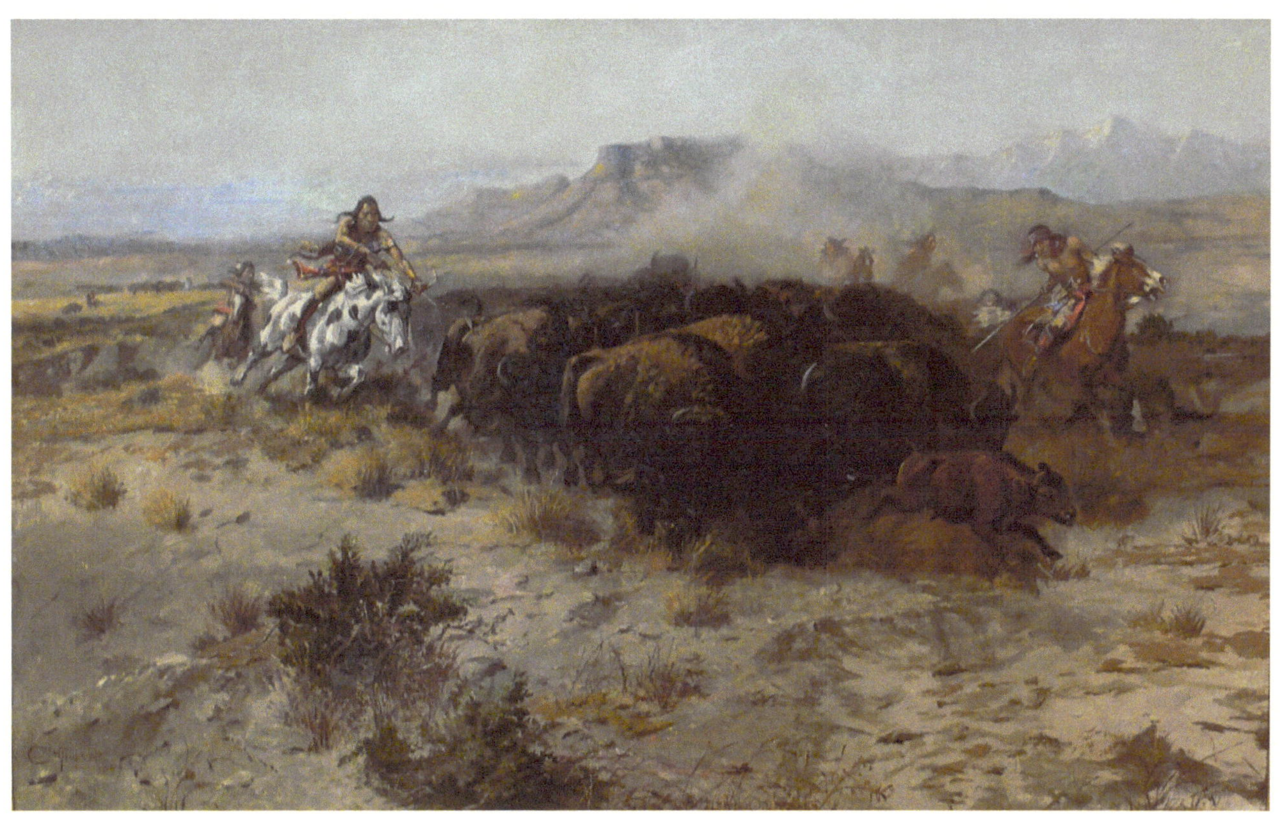

This painting is called Buffalo Hunt. It was painted by Charles M. Russell, who was known for his paintings of cowboys, Indians, and landscapes of the American West.

the Blackfeet. This warlike tribe had not agreed to the peace proposals of Lewis and Clark!

Because of their marvelous trade goods, the whites seemed to have a special kind of power. Who were their spirit helpers? the People wondered. By the 1820s the Nez Perce had heard much about the Christian religion. Did the black book—the Bible—hold the secret to the white men's might? In 1831 four curious Nez Perce men traveled all the way to St. Louis, Missouri, to find out. But the Indians of the Northwest would soon have a chance to learn much more.

CHAPTER TWO

THE WHITE ROAD

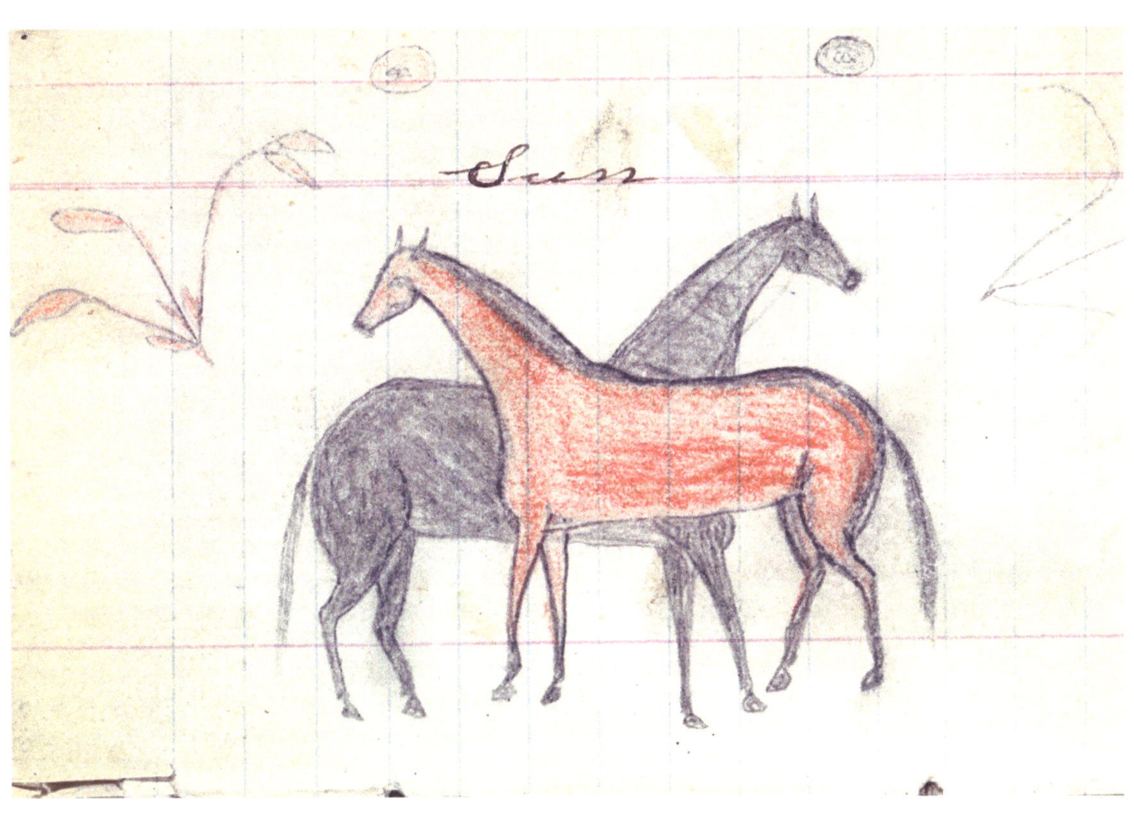

IN 1836 TWO married couples—Marcus and Narcissa Whitman and Henry and Eliza Spalding—came to the Northwest. They were missionaries. Their goal was to convert Indians to Christianity and teach them a "civilized" way of life. The "road of the whites," the Indians called it. The Whitmans settled among the Cayuse tribe. The Spaldings set up their mission in Nez Perce country near the Clearwater River, on Lapwai Creek—"Place of the Butterflies."

At first the Nez Perce welcomed

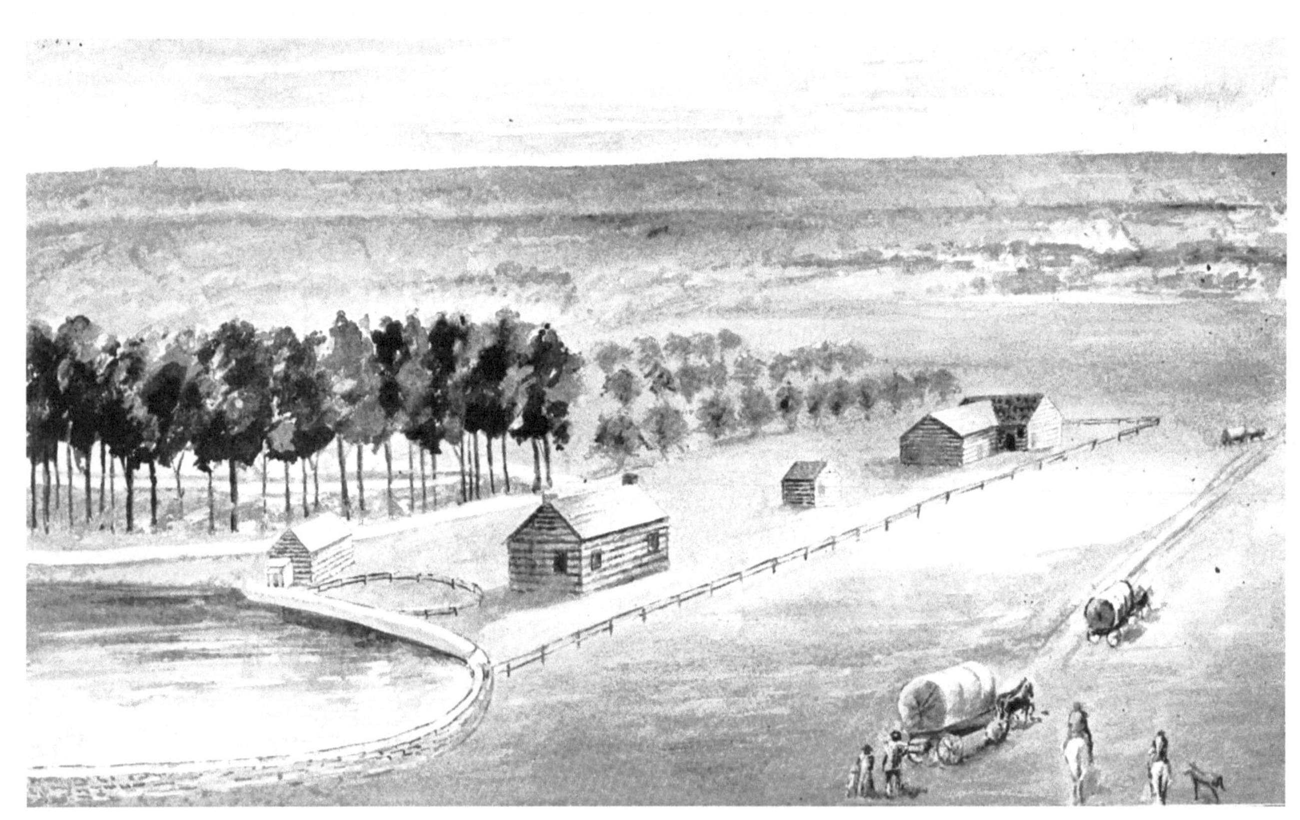

Whitman Mission, 1845

the missionaries and built them a small settlement. They listened to Henry Spalding's harsh sermons. They studied English and Bible stories in Eliza's little school. The missionaries developed a Nez Perce alphabet and printed parts of the Bible in the tribe's own language. Many families moved their tepees close to Lapwai. Spalding showed them how to farm—a practice forbidden by the Dreamer faith.

Old Joseph, then middle-aged, was one of the first of his tribe to become a Christian. For part of the year, he lived at Lapwai. For the rest he went home to the Wallowa.

In that wild country, in 1840, Young Joseph—*Hin-mah-too-ya-lat-kekt*—was born. He was raised in the Nez Perce way, like all the People before him. When he was a tiny baby, his mother carried him in a cradleboard lined with soft animal skin. When she traveled, she hung the cradleboard on her saddle—the baby's first bouncing horseback rides. At age 3, Young Joseph started to ride by himself.

His little brother Ollokot, or "Frog," was born in 1843. The two boys would be loyal and close to each other their whole lives. As they grew they practiced their hunting skills with small bows and arrows. They learned how to catch

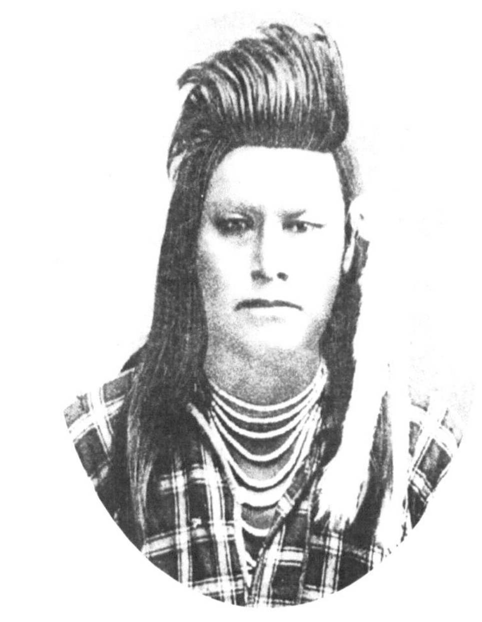

Ollokot, shown here in 1877, looked a lot like his brother, Chief Joseph. He was outgoing and well-liked. Ollokot was a fearless leader in battle.

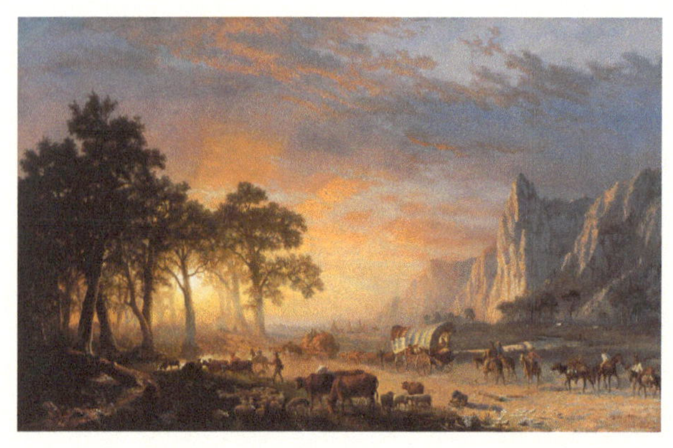

Pioneers traveled to the west on the Oregon Trail. The trail covered about 2000 miles of land.

fish. When they were old enough, they proudly watched over the horse herd. And they raced their ponies with the other boys, galloping over meadows and hills. Above all, the boys learned what it meant to be a Nez Perce: Be brave, be generous, think for yourself, and tell the truth. As their father said, "It was a disgrace to tell a lie."

In these years Old Joseph wanted to combine traditional Indian ways with the best of the white road. So when the family was at Lapwai, Young Joseph and little Ollokot attended Eliza Spalding's school.

But the Indians' world was about to change forever. The same year that Young Joseph was born, the first wagon train rolled west on the Oregon Trail. With each passing year, more pioneers came. Soon there were thousands. "Free land!" cried the Americans back east. "Oregon fever" had broken out.

The Oregon Trail ran close to the Wallowa country, and it cut right through the Whitman mission in the Cayuse homeland. So far, the travelers were not stopping long. They were only passing through on their way to settle on land farther west. But the Cayuse were sure that the Americans would one day try to take their land, too.

Things were going downhill at both missions. Many Indians were angry at the missionaries for trying to make them give up old customs, such as dancing, gambling, and having more than one wife. And they were hearing terrible stories about how tribes in the East had been penned up on reservations. "Kill the whites, or they will destroy you!" warned one man.

Then in 1847 pioneers who were sick with measles stopped at the Whitman mission. Most of the Cayuse caught the disease and fell gravely ill. About half of them died. *Were the whites trying to poison them?* the Indians wondered.

In fear and fury, a group of Cayuse rose up and murdered Marcus and

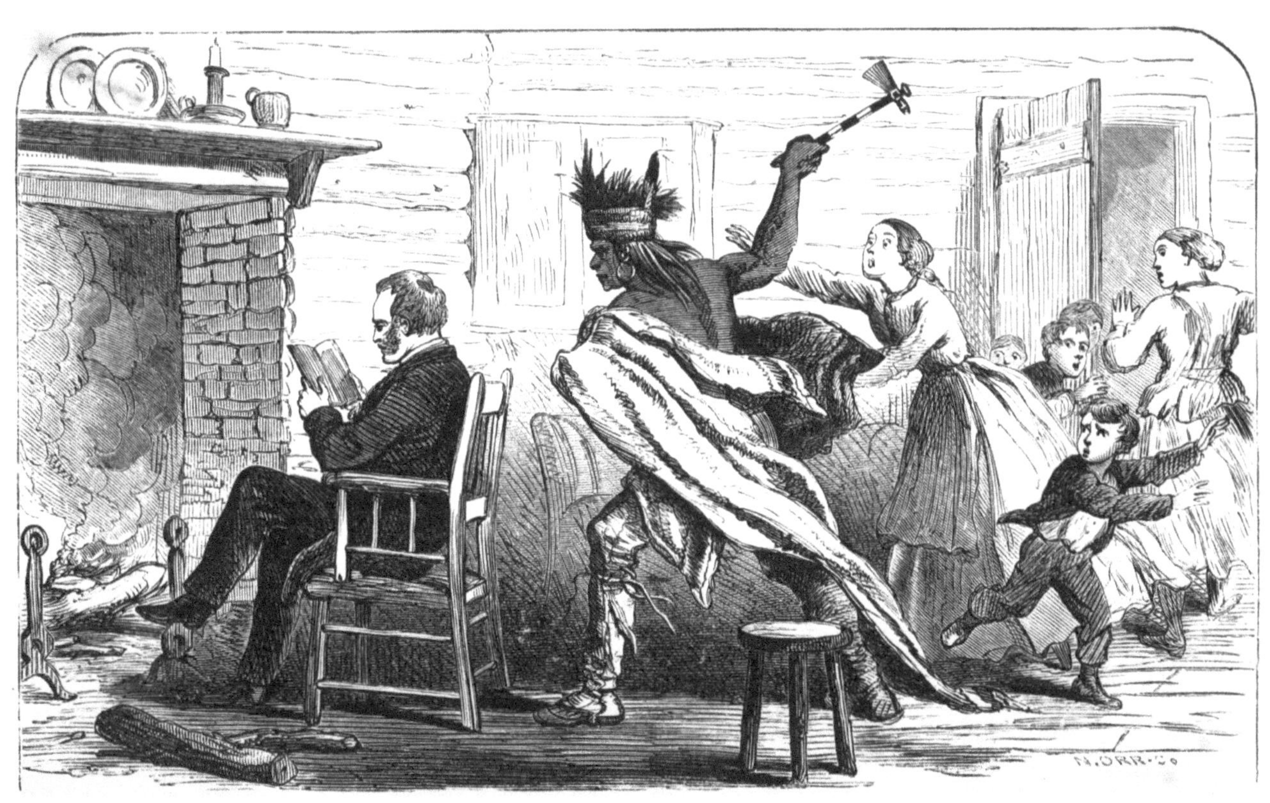

An artist imagines the Cayuse Indian attack on the Whitman mission.

Narcissa Whitman and 11 other white people. When news of the massacre reached the Spalding's settlement, Eliza wrote, "Our only hope is the Nez Perces." They did not let her down. They protected the Spaldings until they could safely leave Indian country.

Soldiers came to punish the Cayuse and nearly destroyed the tribe in a two-year war. Then whites later took over the Cayuse homeland—something they had promised not to do.

Unwilling to be dragged into the fight, the Nez Perce refused to help their friends and relatives, the Cayuse. "I do not want my children engaged in this war," said Old Chief Joseph. Yet he and many others were having deep doubts about their friendship with the Americans. Many Nez Perce were beginning to return to their Dreamer ways.

CHAPTER THREE

YOU INTEND TO WIN OUR COUNTRY

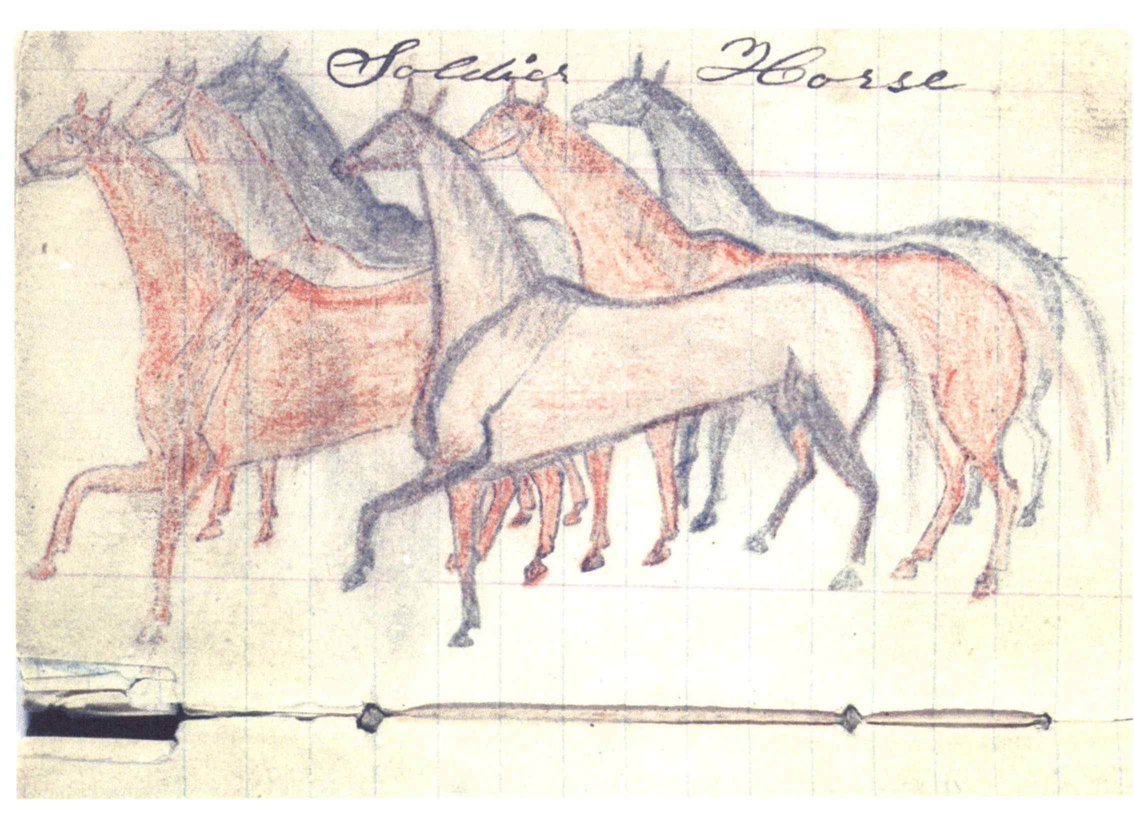

THE COLUMBIA PLATEAU was just one part of a region called for a long time the "Oregon Country." Since 1818 it had been occupied by both Britain and the United States. Then in 1846 the United States gained the whole vast area. Now America stretched from sea to sea—Thomas Jefferson's dream.

By 1853 Congress had divided the old Oregon Country into Oregon Territory and Washington Territory. Now white settlers streamed into the territories because the government was giving away land. Even if Indians already claimed it, American settlers believed it was their "manifest destiny" to fill the continent.

Along came Isaac Stevens, first governor of Washington Territory. He was also in charge of planning the route for a railroad that would run through the Northwest. But before train tracks could be laid, Stevens thought, he had to get the Indians out of the way. He would talk them into signing treaties in which they gave up their land.

In 1855 Stevens and an Oregon official named Joel Palmer called a great council of Indians at the Walla Walla River in Washington Territory. First the Nez Perce rode in, 2,500 strong. Old Chief Joseph brought his son. Young Joseph, then 15 years old. The boy was surely proud of the fine show staged by about 1,000 Nez Perce warriors. They galloped around the council grounds, shooting guns, beating drums, and whooping their loudest war cries.

More tribes of the Columbia Plateau arrived until there were about 5,000 Native Americans in all.

Governor Stevens began by saying, through interpreters, that the "Great Father," the President of the United States, wanted to help his "red children." He wanted to give them money and gifts, everything from frying pans to flourmills. He wanted to give them land for farms of their own. Then, Stevens added, the leftover land would go to the Great Father's "white children."

Joel Palmer told the Indians that they needed protection from the whites. Settlers were coming in great numbers, he said, "like grasshoppers on the plains."

The Indians saw through the friendly talk.

"I think you intend to win our country," said Yellow Bird, a Walla Walla chief.

Yes, the Great Father wanted the Indians to sell their lands and go to reservations.

Hot anger spread among the people.

A Yakima chief spoke: "God made our bodies from the earth... Shall I give the land which is part of my body?"

But, Palmer warned, bad men would take Indian country anyway, if

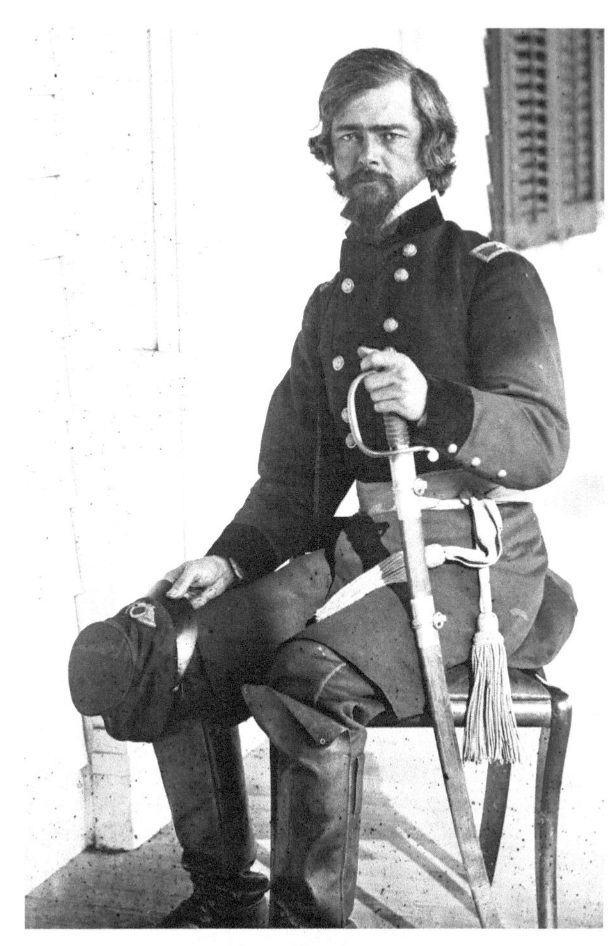

When Isaac Stevens became governor of Washington Territory, he was also given the title Superintendent of Indian Affairs for that region.

the tribes didn't sell it.

Stevens needed the powerful Nez Perce to agree to his plan, so he was ready to give them a special deal. He chose a man named Lawyer to be "head chief" of the whole tribe, even though having one chief to rule over all was not the Nez Perce way. Lawyer could speak English, and he always sided with the whites. He was a "great talker" who worked behind the scenes to push the treaties through.

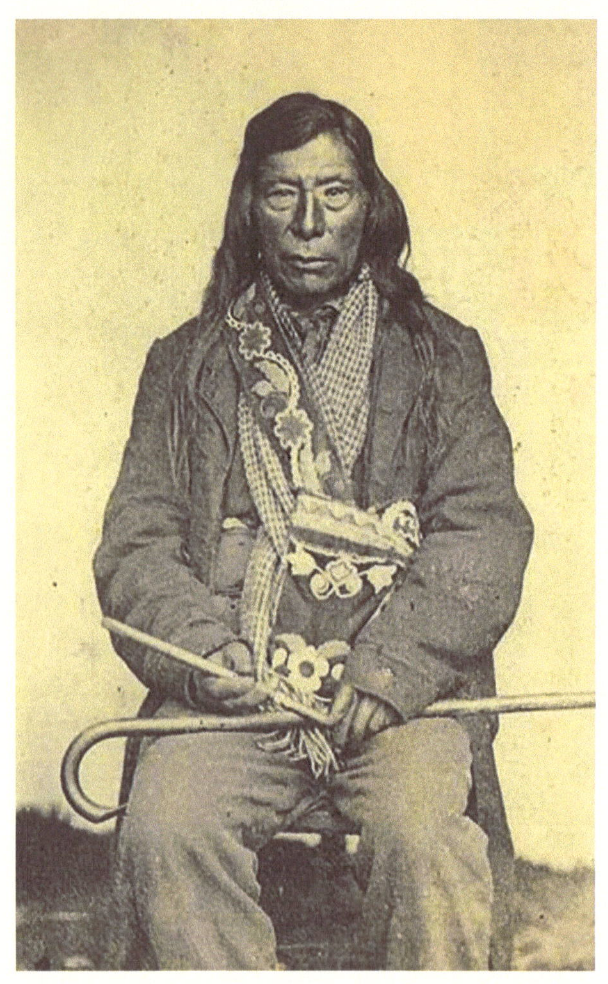

Lawyer was a Nez Perce leader who was in favor of adopting white men's ways.

But Stevens talked more than anybody. Finally he threatened the Indians with force. One by one, the tribes gave in.

There would be three reservations. Only the Nez Perce were satisfied with theirs. They would keep most of their immense country. All 56 Nez Perce chiefs and delegates made their marks—X—on the paper. Old Chief Joseph was among the first to sign. For now the Wallowa country seemed safe.

Just to make sure, Old Chief Joseph made a map of his land. Fie sketched fish to show Wallowa Lake and deer to mark the mountains. Young Joseph and Ollokot probably watched their father draw. They, too, knew their homeland by heart.

But Stevens had truly "won the country" of the other tribes. They would lose most of their land and be crowded onto the other two reservations. One Yakima chief was so angry when he signed the treaty that he bit his lip until it bled.

Stevens had promised that no whites could enter Indian country until the treaties were approved by Congress. But he broke this promise right away and declared the lands "open for settlement." Soon miners and settlers began pouring in.

The Plateau Indians knew they had been tricked, and they fought back. War raged in the Northwest until 1858, when the United States Army crushed the rebellion. Many Indians, even those who had surrendered, were hanged. When the 1855 treaties were finally approved in 1859, the defeated tribes went to their reservations.

Once again the Nez Perce had refused to help the other Indians. They did not want soldiers coming to their land. But now they argued among themselves. Some, like Lawyer, were Christians and farmers. They believed that in order to survive, they would always have to please the powerful whites. Some in this group had actually helped the army during the Plateau wars. Others, like Old Joseph, were sorry that they had signed the treaty. They only wanted to be left alone.

The Nez Perce still had their land, but the Americans were crowding ever closer. Old Joseph worried about the future. As he had said at the treaty council, "It is not for us we talk, it is for our children who come after us."

CHAPTER FOUR

THIEF TREATY

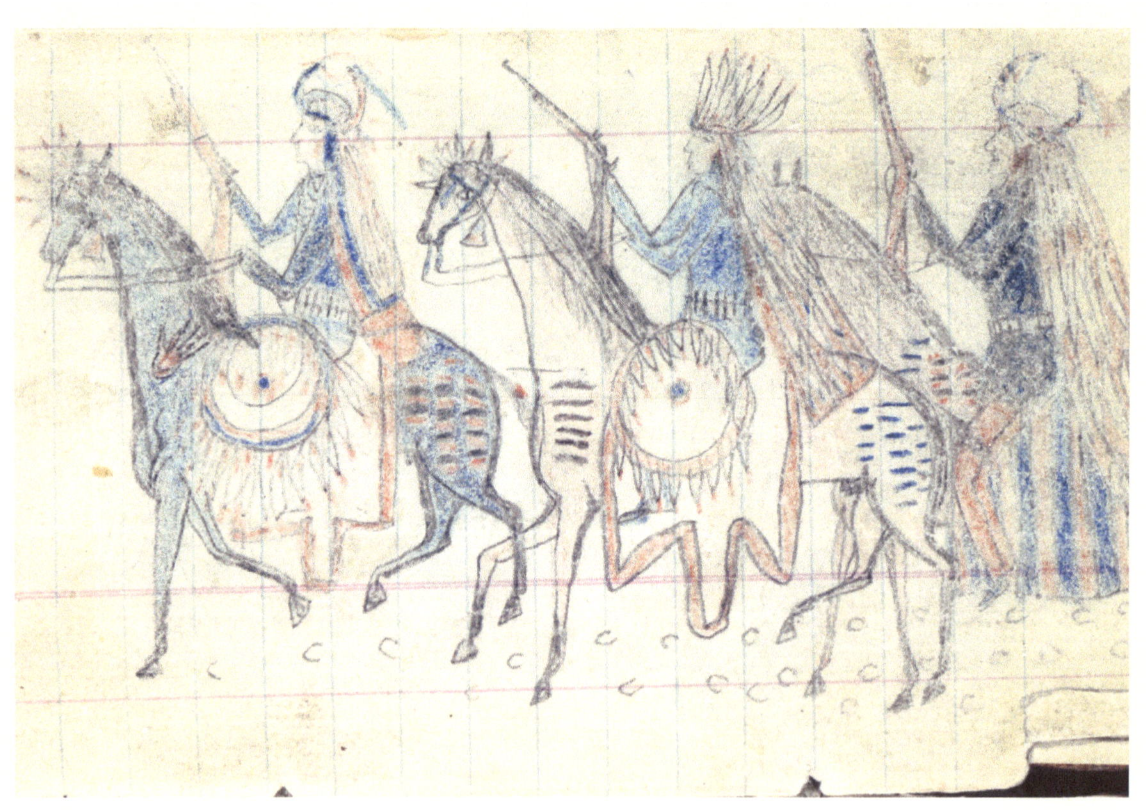

GOLD! IN 1860 a miner named Ellas Pierce spotted flakes of the glittering metal in a stream near the Clearwater River in Idaho. Word traveled fast. Soon thousands of men came, hoping to strike it rich. But they were invading the Nez Perce Reservation. According to the Treaty of 1855, no whites were allowed on tribal lands without permission from the chiefs. The reservation agency, or headquarters, was at Lapwai Creek, on the site of the old Spalding mission. A military post. Fort Lapwai, was built nearby. Yet neither the government agent nor the soldiers at the fort could stop the swarm of miners. They were like a "whirlwind," wrote one man.

The miners built wagon roads and towns. They cut down trees and stole livestock. They sold whiskey to the Indians, upsetting family life. They also robbed and murdered an unknown number of Nez Perce. And they were not punished for it.

Some of the Nez Perce sold food to the miners. They also made money by ferrying the white men across the rivers. But the Dreamer chiefs in the Salmon River country tried to drive out the invaders. "Look here," the chiefs were told, "for every white man you kill, a thousand will take his place." The Dreamers saw that this was true, so they did not make war.

The map of the Northwest was still changing fast. Oregon became a state in 1859. The Wallowa country was inside its borders. In 1863, Congress established Idaho Territory—gold had made the region famous. Now the Nez Perce reservation stretched over three separate parts of the United States—Idaho, Oregon, and Washington. Since politicians wanted more land for the growing numbers of settlers, they decided that the reservation would have to be made smaller.

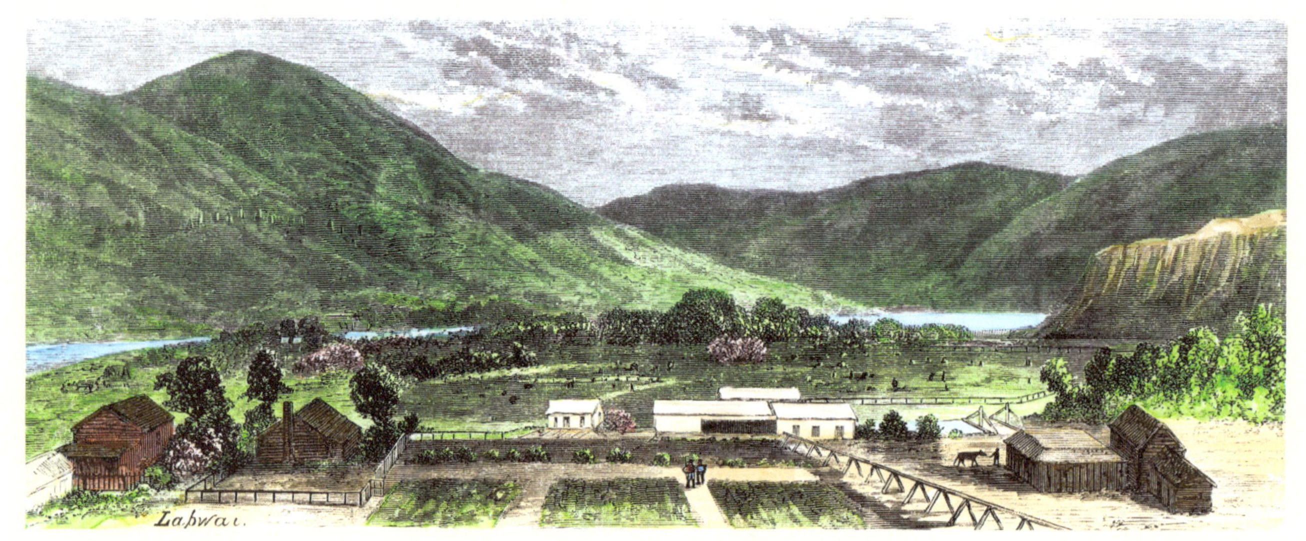

Farms at Lapwai

In 1863 a treaty council was held at Fort Lapwai. Calvin Hale, Superintendent of Indian Affairs in Washington Territory, was in charge. Almost the whole Nez Perce tribe—about 3,000 in all—came to hear him. There were the "Lawyer people"—Christians and farmers—who lived along the Clearwater. And there were the Dreamers, with their leaders White Bird, Looking Glass, Big Thunder, Eagle-from-the-Light, Toohoolhoolzote, and Old Joseph. Young Joseph and Ollokot, now 23 and 20 years old, were there, too.

The Nez Perce listened to Hale in a state of shock. He wanted them to sell most of their reservation—for $265,000. The government planned to reduce Nez Perce country to one tenth its current size! It would shrink from 7 million acres to 700,000. Hale would take away the Wallowa country. And he would take away almost all the rest of Nez Perce land. The whole tribe would be crowded onto a new, smaller reservation around Lapwai. This was land that already belonged to Lawyer and his followers.

At first even Lawyer was against it. He complained that the tribe had seen almost none of the goods promised in the Treaty of 1855. Another man said, "It does not look good; it looks crooked...we cannot sell our country." But it soon appeared that Lawyer and his men would give in. Hale was secretly promising them special payments and benefits. And after all, they would lose none of their own land.

Under a big tent, the Nez Perce alone held an all-night meeting. There the Christians and the Dreamers agreed to split the tribe into two groups—"treaty" and "nontreaty" Indians. The Nez Perce people, once so strong, were now divided forever.

The Dreamers, or Nontreaties, stood firm. They would sell nothing, they said. They went home before the council was over. But when they were gone. Lawyer and other treaty men signed Hale's papers. They sold land that did not belong to them. "Sold our country which they did not own," said Young Joseph's cousin. Yellow Wolf.

The nontreaty Nez Perce called this document the "Thief Treaty." When Old Joseph received his copy, he tore it to pieces. He also ripped up his Bible, a gift from Henry Spalding. All the whites had ever wanted, he now believed, was to steal his country. Then he placed tall poles around the boundary of his land. They were a warning to the settlers to keep out.

For the next few years, the nontreaty bands ignored the Treaty of 1863. They kept on living in the old way as much as possible. Chief White Bird's people hung on to the Salmon River country, already filling up with miners

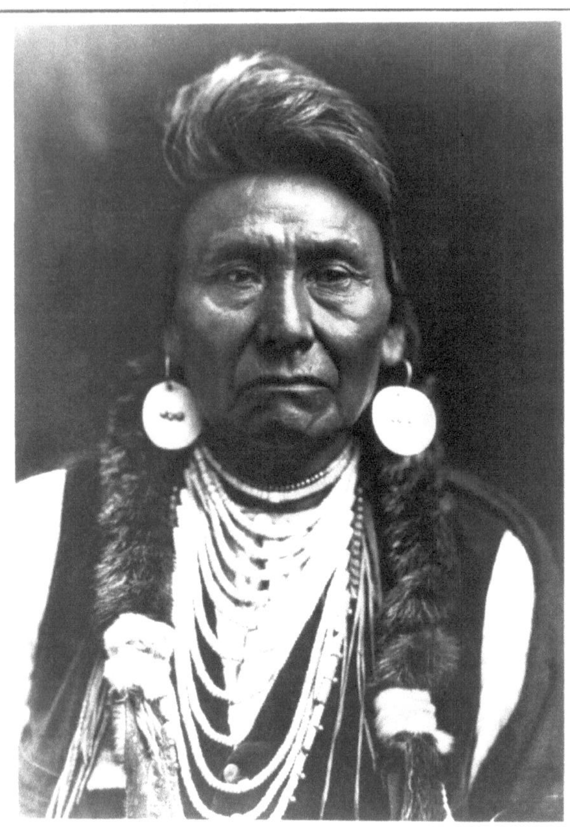

Chief Joseph has been honored with many present-day namesakes, including Joseph, Oregon; Chief Joseph Pass in Montana; and Chief Joseph Elementary School in Meridian, Idaho.

and settlers. Chief Looking Glass and his band lived by the Middle Fork of the Clearwater. Toohoolhoolzote led a small group in the rugged land between the Salmon and the Snake. And there was Old Joseph's band of about 200 people, safe so far, in the high Wallowa.

But just before he died in 1871, Old Joseph warned, "A few years more, and white men will be all around you." That year Young Joseph became Chief Joseph, the youngest of the nontreaty chiefs. Ollokot, a splendid hunter and fighter, was to serve as the Wallowa's war chief.

The new Chief Joseph, now 31, was tall and handsome. While many of the Christian Nez Perce cut their hair short and dressed like white men, Joseph followed the Dreamer style of his band. His long braids were wrapped in strips of fur. The hair in front was cut short and made to stick straight up from his forehead. His moccasins were of soft deerskin. Shell earrings dangled from his ears, and he wore many strands of shells and beads around his neck.

Now he had a wife named Bear Crossing and a young daughter, Kapkap Ponmi, or Sound of Running Feet. Joseph was well suited to being chief. Like his father he was thoughtful and serious, with a dignified manner. He was a quiet man, but when he spoke, it was with spirit and passion.

Right away he had trouble on his hands. The year his father died, settlers began coming, at last, to the valley. They brought their horses and cattle to graze on the rich Wallowa grasslands. They built cabins for their families. To American ranchers, Chief Joseph's land looked like heaven on earth.

CHAPTER FIVE

IT WILL HAVE TO BE WAR!

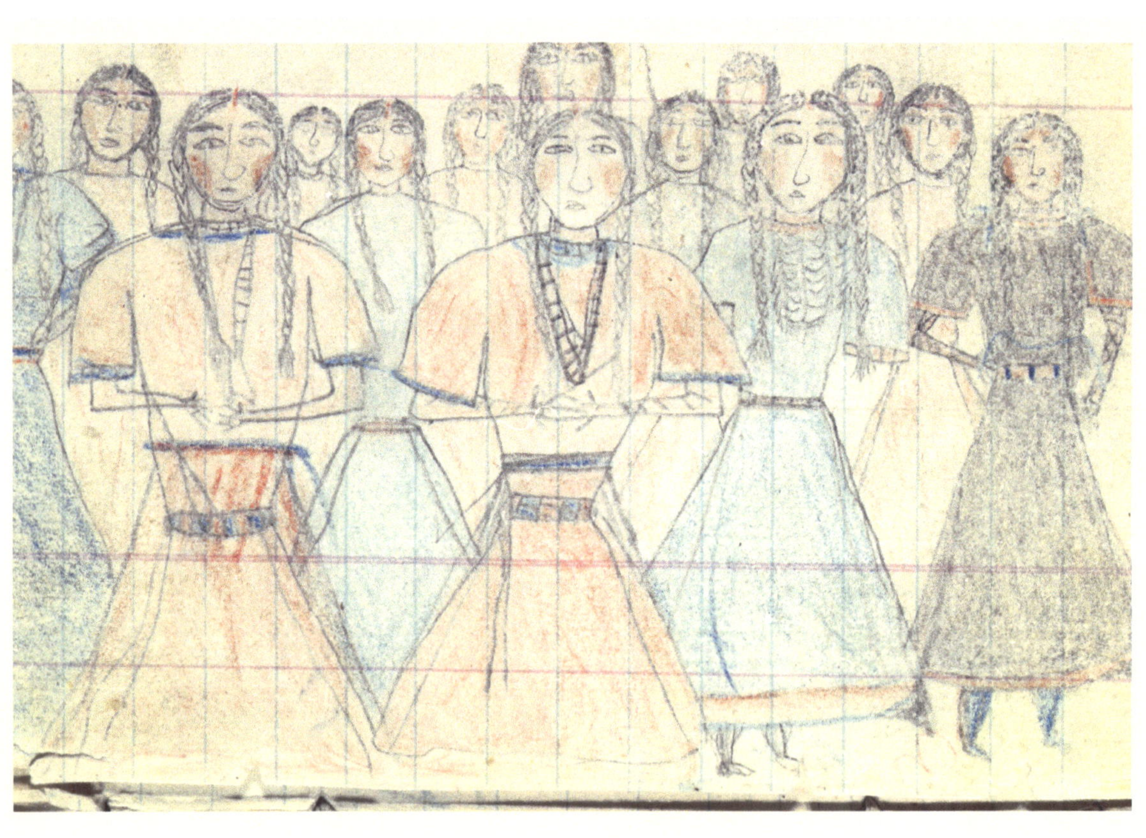

CHIEF JOSEPH SPOKE up to protect his home. Firmly he told the intruders that the Wallowas had never sold their country. *The settlers must go.* But they refused to leave. They told Joseph that, according to the Treaty of 1863, the Indians *had* sold their land. *It was the Nez Perce who must go—to the Lapwai reservation.*

Bad feelings between Indians and whites grew. Some of the ranchers stole Nez Perce livestock and claimed ever more land for their herds. Chief Joseph wanted peace. But, he said, "The white man would not let us alone." He began an endless round of talks with settlers and government officials. Over and over he explained that the Treaty of 1863 had been a terrible trick.

Joseph talked several times with John Monteith, the agent at Lapwai. At first Monteith sided with the Wallowa band. "It is a great pity that the Valley was ever opened for settlement," he wrote. Other officials agreed.

In 1873, President Ulysses S. Grant ordered that half of the valley be set aside for Joseph's people. But this made Oregon's politicians furious, so Grant's order was not carried out. Monteith, under pressure, now sided with the settlers.

Chief Joseph did not give up.

In 1875 he met for the first time with General Oliver Otis Howard, the general in charge of military matters for much of the Northwest. Howard had fought bravely during the Civil War. Because he had lost his right arm in battle, the Nez Perce would call him "Cut Arm." A devout Christian, Howard believed himself to be a fair-minded man. He listened to Joseph and decided that the chief was right. The Indians had never sold their valley.

It seemed to Joseph that he was finally winning. Then President

Grant took back his order, a move that General Howard called a "great mistake."

To make matters worse, in the spring of 1876, a friend of Joseph's—a man named Wind Blowing—was murdered by two settlers. The settlers were not punished. Anger among the Wallowas was about to boil over. Joseph had a hard time controlling his young warriors, who were eager for revenge.

In November Joseph appeared before a five-man commission set up by the Indian Bureau in Washington, D.C. General Howard was one of the five. But Howard, too, had changed his mind about the Wallowa band. Now he threatened Joseph with force if his people refused to leave the valley. Once again Joseph was firm. The land, he said, was "too sacred to be...sold for silver and gold."

But the commissioners had made up their minds even before they heard Joseph speak. They urged the Indian Bureau to put all the nontreaty bands on the reservation. When Joseph heard this, he could hardly believe his ears. "I Have been talking to the whites for many years about the land in question, and it is strange that they cannot understand me. ...I will not leave it until I am compelled to." Ollokot asked Howard for one more meeting. It was the band's last chance.

On May 3, 1877, Joseph and Ollokot led a large group of Wallowas to Fort Lapwai to meet with Howard and Monteith. In they rode on horses decorated with feathers and bright paint. Their own faces were painted red. They wore their best beaded clothes and finest blankets. And they were singing—singing to show their strength. The other nontreaty bands arrived led by White Bird, Looking Glass, and Toohoolhoolzote. Bald

Head and Hahtalekin, chiefs of the small Palouse tribe came, too. The Palouse, who lived by the Snake River, had also refused to move to Lapwai. But all the chiefs agreed: They did not want war with the United States. It was a war they could not win.

Toohoolhoolzote spoke first. He told Howard that the People must not be parted from the earth, their mother. It did not matter what papers the treaty Indians had signed.

Howard was stern with the people he called "savages." He especially disliked Toohoolhoolzote because he was a leading Dreamer. The general said, "...twenty times over I hear that the earth is your mother...I want to hear it no more, but come to business at once." And he told the bands that troops were ready to force them to Lapwai.

Toohoolhoolzote was proud and bitter: "I am telling you! I am a chief! Who can tell me what I must do in my own country?"

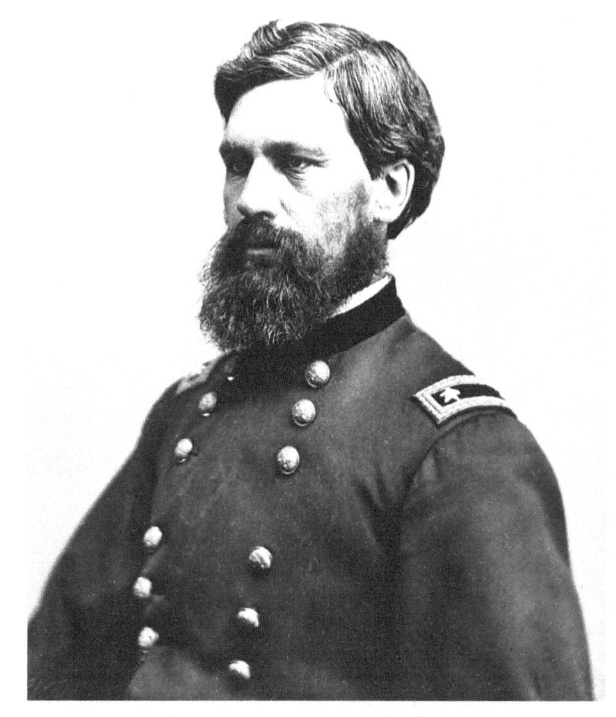

General Oliver Otis Howard

"I am the man to tell you what you must do!" shouted Howard. "You will come on the reservation. ... If not, soldiers will put you there or shoot you down!"

"I will not leave my home, the land where I grew up!"

Howard threw Toohoolhoolzote into the guardhouse, where he would stay for the rest of the council.

Then Joseph spoke but also got nowhere. Soldiers with rifles gathered closer. Now the chiefs heard that troops were already in the Wallowa Valley. The Nez Perce were trapped. To save the lives of their families, they agreed to choose land on the reservation. As Joseph said of the whites, "We were like deer. They were like grizzly bears."

It was May 14. Howard gave the bands only 30 days, until June 14, to move to Lapwai. And not one day more, he warned.

It was a cruel order, too short a time for such a move. Heavy with grief, the Wallowa women loaded as much as they could on pack horses. They would have to leave many belongings behind. Men and boys roamed the countryside, gathering their scattered herds. It was impossible to find them all. In early June, Joseph's people left their ancient home.

Next they had to cross the Snake River. At this time of year, it was roaring with snowmelt from the mountains. The water teemed with whirlpools and rapids. But the Nez Perce knew the river well. After loading "bullboats," they sat on top of their piled-up possessions. Then men and horses pulled the boats across, making many trips back and forth. The Indians drove thousands of their horses and cattle into the river, but hundreds never made it to the other side. The weakest ones—the youngest and oldest—drowned in the rushing water. When the band came to the Salmon River, they had to cross it the same way. This time they left their cattle behind.

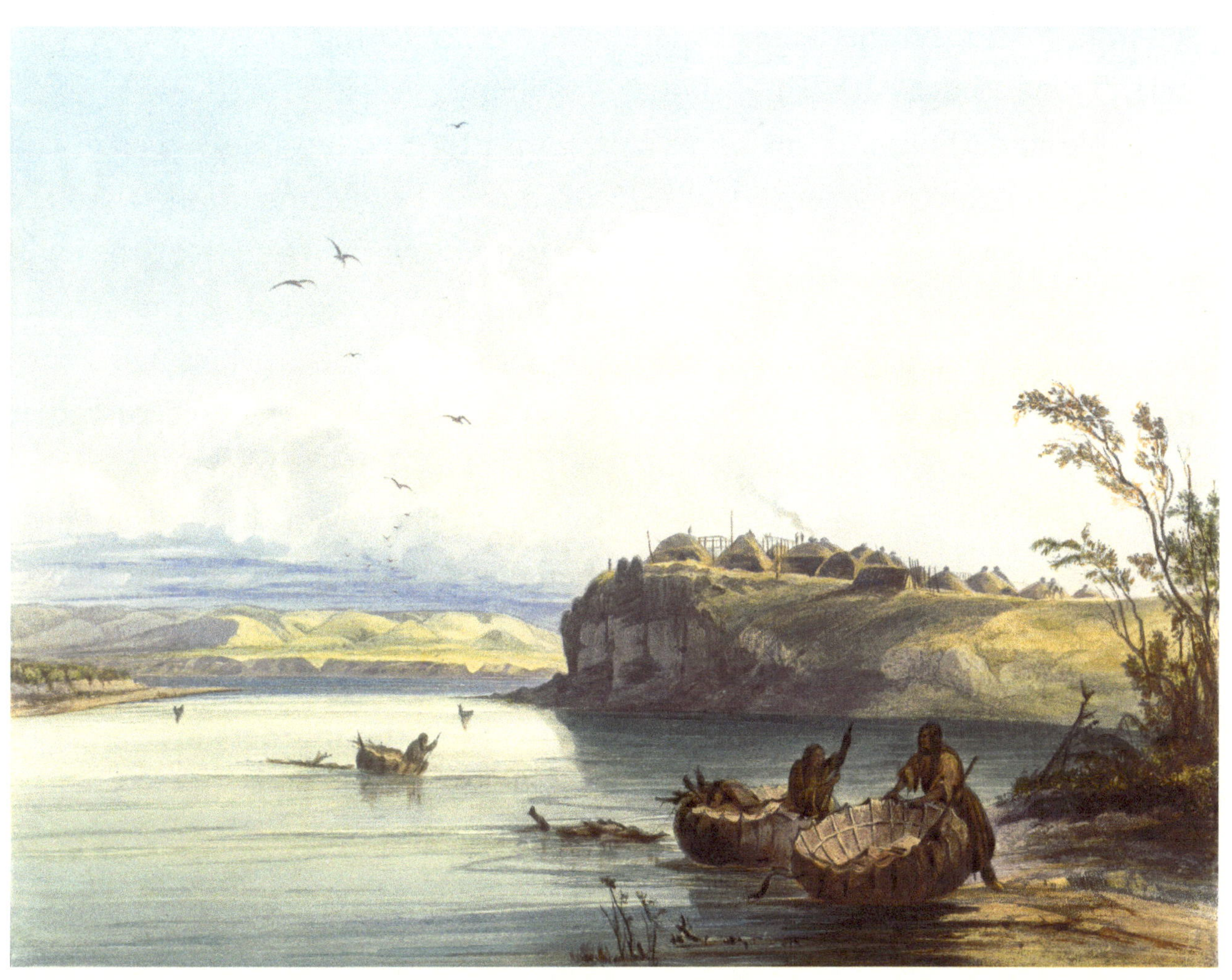

The Nez Perce made round "bullboats"out of willow branches and buffalo hides. The boats allowed them to cross even the swiftest rivers.

The Wallowas joined the other nontreaty bands at a campground called Split Rocks, on the wide Camas Prairie. It was a huge gathering, about 700 people and thousands of horses. At Split Rocks, Joseph's second wife. Springtime, gave birth to a baby girl. And there, too, the People tried to enjoy their last days of freedom. Warriors painted their faces, put on feathered war bonnets, and held a big parade.

During the parade someone mocked a young man named Shore Crossing because he had not killed the white man who had murdered his father. Eagle Robe, years earlier. Shore Crossing could not stand being called a coward. With two friends, he quietly left camp, looking for revenge.

On June 13 and 14, the three friends rode along the Salmon River valley. They never found Eagle Robe's killer, but they shot four other white men. Soon another war party from Split Rocks joined them. The young men all went on a killing spree, shooting and stabbing at least 12 settlers.

In 1805 the Nez Perce had promised Lewis and Clark that they would always be friends of the white men. For 70 years the Indians had kept their promise. They had kept it even though since the gold rush days, whites had killed about 30 members of their tribe. Even worse, the People had been robbed of their homeland. The anger of their young men had finally exploded.

News of the murders arrived at the Nez Perce camp just as men in council were discussing whether to go to the reservation or fight. Someone shouted out, "You poor people are holding council for nothing! … It will have to be war!" The United States Army was sure to strike back.

CHAPTER SIX

THEY WERE HOMELESS

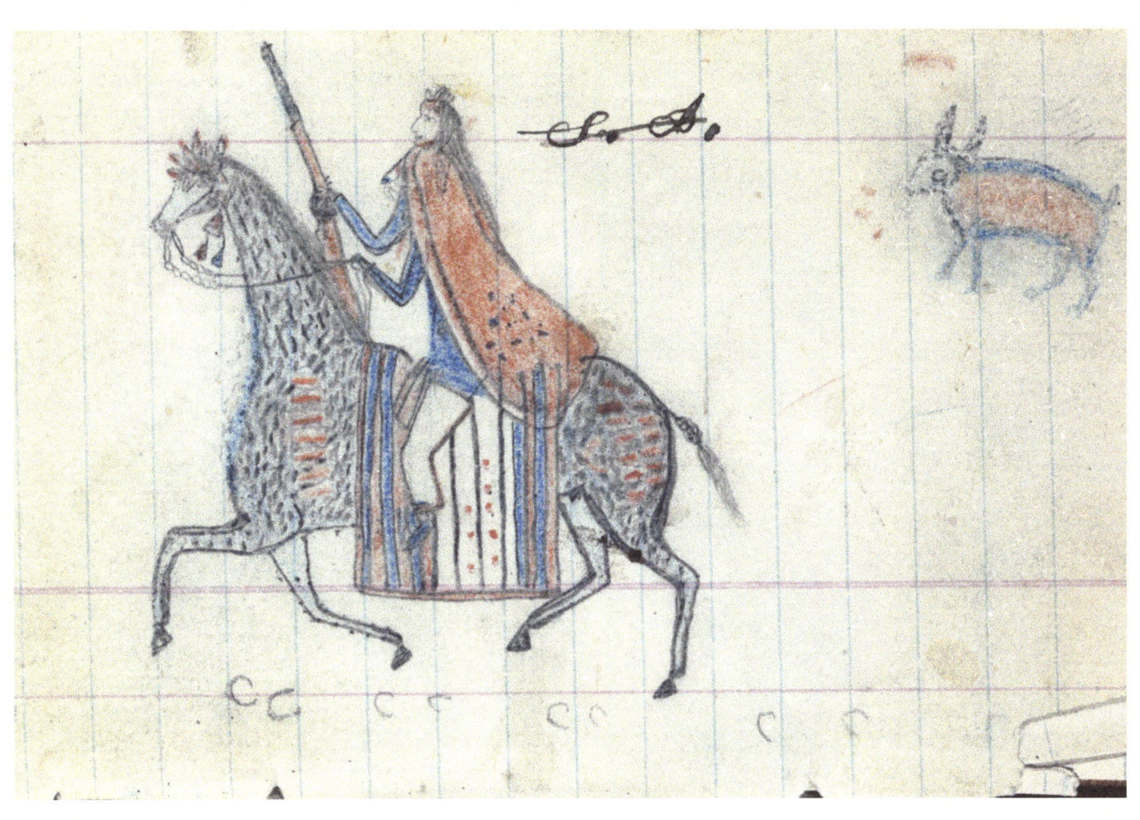

CHIEF JOSEPH HAD lost his valley. Now, with war coming, he might lose his family and friends to the soldiers' bullets. "I would have given my own life if I could have undone the killing of white men by my people," he said.

After the Salmon River murders. Looking Glass and his band returned to their village on the Clearwater River. Their Palouse relatives went with them. But the other nontreaty bands rode a few miles south to camp at White Bird Creek, at the bottom of the deep White Bird Canyon. The campsite was well protected, with steep hills in front and the Salmon River behind. There the Indians waited. Chief Joseph and others still hoped that somehow they could step back into peace.

Back at Lapwai, General Howard heard about the killing spree. He had thought that the bands were quietly heading to the reservation. Instead, panic was spreading like fire through the countryside. Settlers rushed to the little towns of Grangeville and Mount Idaho for protection. Surely, they thought, they were in the middle of an all-out Indian war. They begged Howard for help: "Hurry up; hurry!"

Howard sprang into action. He telegraphed throughout the Northwest for troops and supplies. And he sent Captain David Perry, with about 90 cavalry men—"horse soldiers," the Indians called them—to put down the uprising. Then Howard sent a message to his army superior. General Irvin McDowell: "Think they will make short work of it."

Perry's troops reached the edge of White Bird Canyon dead tired after a 70-mile ride. With them was a group of citizens who had volunteered to fight. The volunteers told the soldiers not to worry, because the Nez Perce were cowards, easy to beat. The

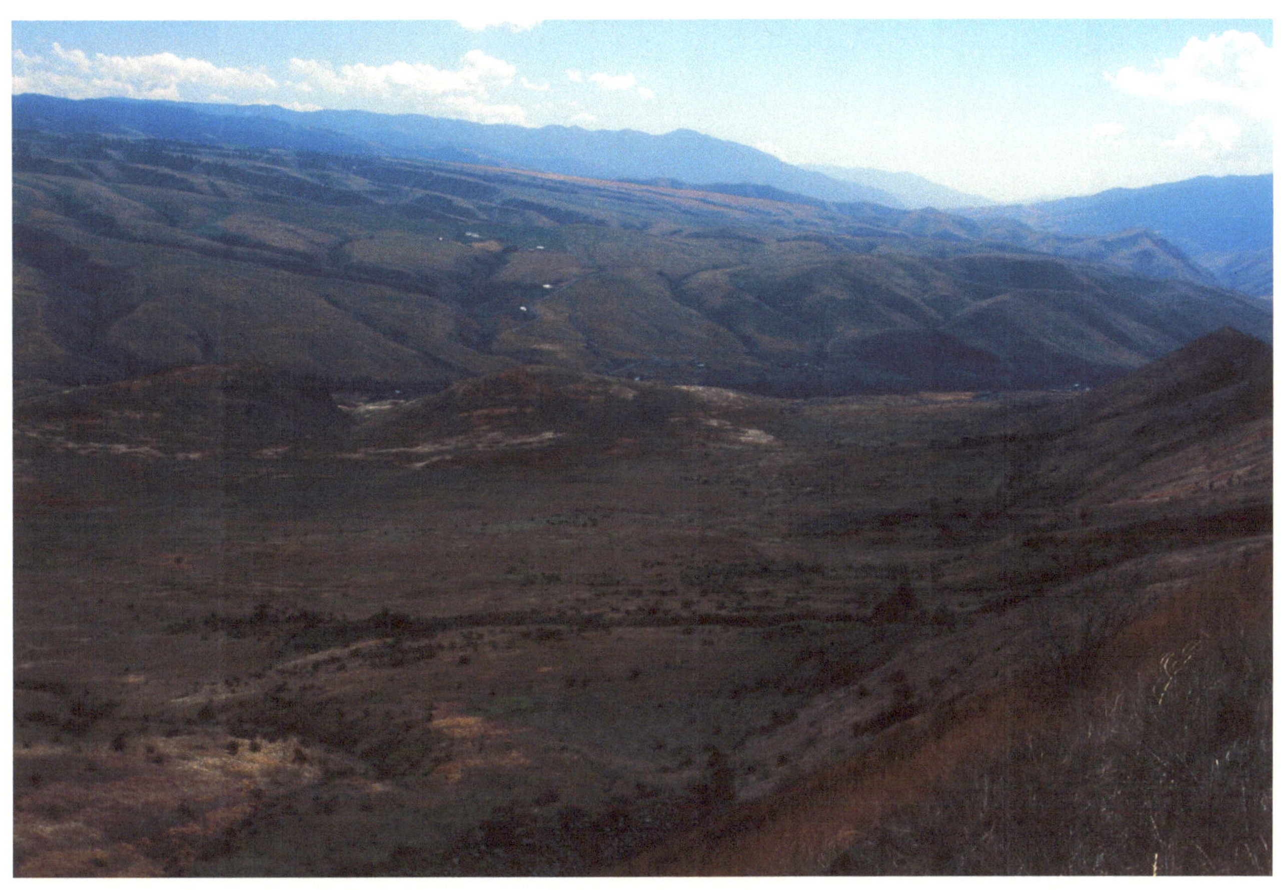

White Bird battlefield

captain planned a dawn attack. But in the chilly hours before sunrise on June 17, the men heard the haunting howl of a coyote. It wasn't a real coyote, they knew. It was an Indian, warning his people that soldiers were near. Perry's surprise had been ruined.

At dawn the troops started down the slope toward the Nez Perce camp. A volunteer named Ad Chapman, a white man who had married an Indian, led the way. Suddenly, up from the

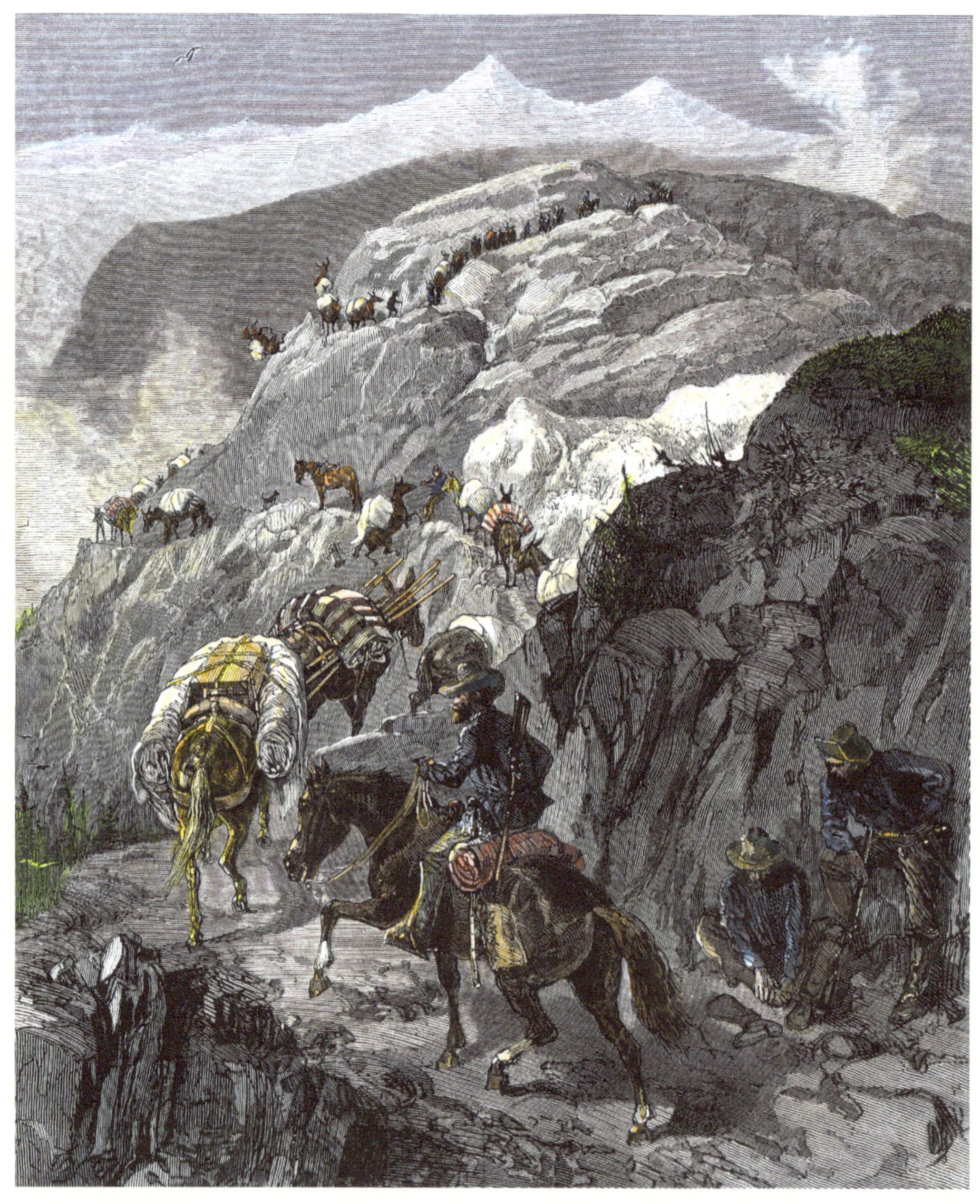

General Howard pursuing the Nez Perce Indians, with a long train of mules

camp rode a party of warriors, holding the white flag of truce. It was their last attempt to avoid war. But Chapman fired his gun. Within seconds a Nez Perce shot Captain Perry's trumpeter. Now Perry would have no way to signal commands to his men. The Nez Perce War of 1877 had begun.

About 60 warriors were stripped to their breechcloths and painted for war. Out from their hiding places on the sides of the canyon they galloped. Two Moons and Ollokot led the young men as they swirled among the troops, leaping off their ponies to shoot, and attacking from every direction. They struck so fast that the troops hardly saw them coming. The Indians had only outdated guns and bows and arrows, but they were expert marksmen. They almost always hit their targets. It was a short battle. Cavalry horses stampeded. Soldiers panicked and ran, and the warriors chased them for about 12 miles.

The Battle of White Bird Canyon was a stunning victory for the Indians. They killed 34 soldiers and gathered much-needed guns and ammunition from the battlefield. Not a single Nez Perce died. Now a dismayed General Howard called for troops from as far away as Alaska and Georgia. He blamed the army's defeat on Joseph. Before the war the chief had spoken so forcefully for his land that Howard thought he must be the tribe's war leader, too. Throughout the country, Americans heard bloody tales about "Chief Joseph's War."

General Howard and the newspapers were wrong. Joseph, now 37, fought along with the other men. But he was not a famed warrior. His main job was that of camp chief. In the coming months, he would be in charge of the families, helping them to move camp and gather their horses.

He would guide the people on the long trails ahead.

There would be no permanent war chief among the Nez Perce. A council of chiefs, elders, and warriors would meet during the war to choose new leaders when necessary. Together they would make other important decisions. Unlike soldiers in the United States Army, Nez Perce fighters did not have to follow orders. They could fight in their own way. They could even leave the battlefield if they chose. But during this crisis, worse than anything they had ever faced, the Nez Perce would stick together. It was for the good of the People.

After White Bird Canyon, there was no turning back. The Nez Perce crossed the Salmon River and waited for the army that was sure to return. On June 26, General Howard himself came, with about 500 men. Some of Howard's scouts were treaty Nez Perce, friendly to the whites. A long "train" of mules carried the army's supplies. Howard also brought powerful, horse-drawn weapons—two Gatling guns (early machine guns), and a type of cannon. First he stopped to bury the soldiers killed in the White Bird fight. Then he, too, crossed the river. This took four days, since his men did not know how to make bullboats. The soldiers wondered. How had the Indians scooted over so quickly, with all their belongings and horses?

Now the Indians led Howard on a maddening chase. As soon as the troops crossed the Salmon, the bands crossed back again to the other side. Howard's men were left far behind, hiking hungry and wet on the wrong side of the river. The Indians thought of a new name for Cut-Arm—"General Day-After-Tomorrow."

They headed east across Camas Prairie. Warriors scouted in front, behind, and all around the families to keep them safe. A war party led by Rainbow and Five Wounds, two great Nez Perce warriors, spotted soldiers camped in the distance. Soon a group of 13 came riding their way.

The Indians sang their war songs. They called on their spirit powers for help. Then they ambushed the 13 men, killing every one. Later the Nez Perce had a firefight with a group of volunteers who had come to help the soldiers. In this clash three volunteers would die and one Indian. He was the first Nez Perce to be killed in the war. But the families had crossed the prairie unharmed.

Onward they went, with their horse herd and pack horses and watchful warriors on every side. On July 6 the bands camped on the South Fork of the Clearwater River. They were overjoyed when Looking Class's people and some from the Palouse tribe joined them. Now the bands numbered about 200 warriors and almost 550 old men, women, and children.

A week earlier soldiers had gone to Looking Glass's village to arrest the chief and his people. There were rumors that the band was secretly

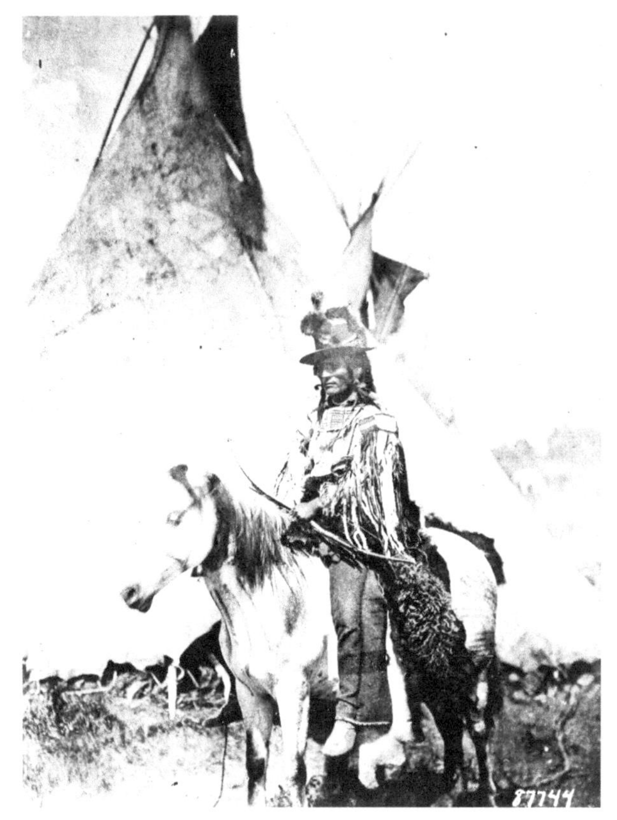

Chief Looking Glass

helping the "hostiles," as the army called the fighting Nez Perce. In fact, Looking Glass wanted nothing to do with the war. But the whites started shooting. As Indians ran for their lives, soldiers burned the village and stole hundreds of ponies. "Now, my people," said Looking Glass, "as long as I live, I will never make peace with the treacherous Americans. ... I am ready for war."

Meanwhile General Howard was nearing his enemy again. On July 11, as the army marched along the bluffs overlooking the Clearwater, one man spied the Nez Perce camp far below. Immediately the general opened fire with his big guns. Then he sent the soldiers down toward the camp.

The Indians were caught by surprise. They had fewer than a hundred warriors. But once again they blocked the soldiers' charge. Toohoolhoolzote, old but still fierce, led a war party that rushed up the rocky slope into enemy fire. Rainbow, Five Wounds, and Ollokot led others. The Nez Perce fought in the Indian way, in small groups or alone, taking cover behind rocks and bushes. Yellow Wolf, now a daring 21-year-old brave, remembered that "bullets were singing like bees."

It was a hot, thirsty day and a long night. Neither side gained ground. By the second day, many warriors had grown tired of the standstill. One by one they began to leave the battlefield. Now Howard's guns boomed into the village. Chief Joseph hurried to move the families out. The soldiers charged the camp on the heels of the fleeing Indians. The families reached safety, but many of their possessions had been left behind. "Burn everything!" the soldiers were ordered.

General Howard claimed a big victory. But he had lost 13 men, and only 4 Nez Perce had died. Yellow Wolf said later, "But we were not whipped! Had we been whipped, we could not have escaped from there with our lives."

The People hurried across the river to Weippe Prairie. Here, where their forefathers had welcomed Lewis and Clark, the Indians held a solemn council. Looking Glass was chosen war chief of all the bands. He wanted to lead the families over the mountains to Montana's buffalo country, where the Grow Indians would surely help them. "The Grows are the same as my brothers," he said. Chief Joseph preferred to stay and fight in Nez Perce country. But the council chose Looking Glass's plan. The people were now in flight from their own land. "They were homeless and desperate," Joseph said. And he would go with them wherever they had to go.

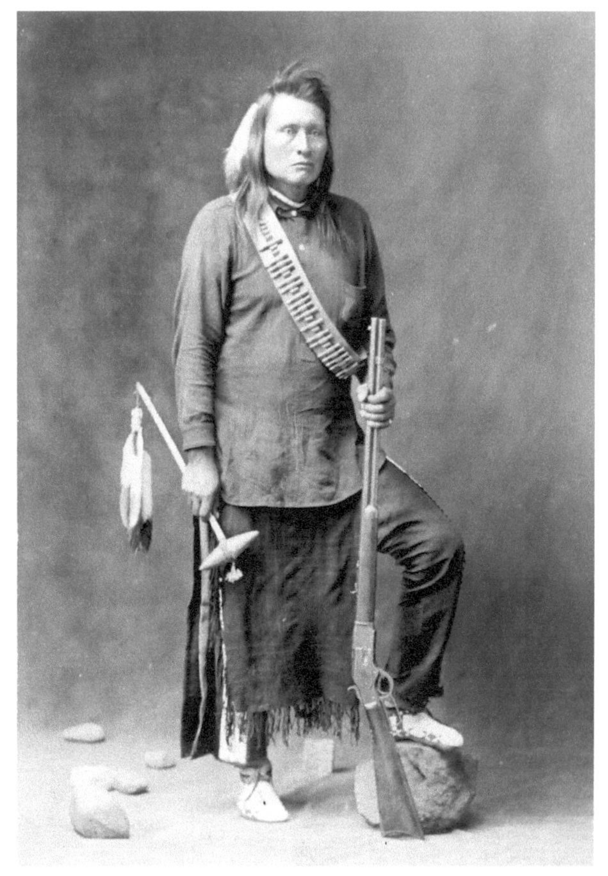

Yellow Wolf, many years after the Nez Perce war

CHAPTER SEVEN

FROM THE LOLO TRAIL TO THE BIG HOLE

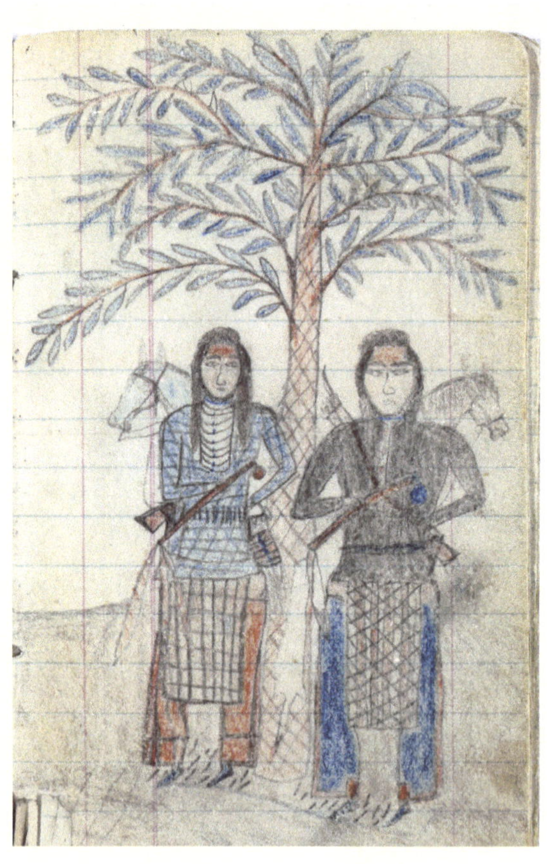

MORE THAN 700 Nez Perce, with 2,000 horses, headed to Montana on the Lolo Trail. The Lolo was 100 miles long and very steep—a jumble of logs, rocks, and deep ravines. Pack horses fell off the trail or broke bones as they scrambled over boulders. In their flight the Indians left many crippled and dead animals behind. The path was marked with their blood.

Back in Idaho, General Howard was ordered by William Tecumseh Sherman, the army's top general, to follow the hostiles wherever they went. Howard ordered more supplies and gathered a force of about 700 men. This included Indians who were willing to help. Some were treaty Nez Perce. Some were Bannock Indians, old enemies of the Nez Perces. They hoped to capture Nez Perce horses.

Howard had telegraphed ahead for support from troops in Montana. Captain Charles Rawn, commander of an army post there, hurried to help. With soldiers and volunteers, Rawn built a log barricade across the Montana end of the Lolo Trail. Also in

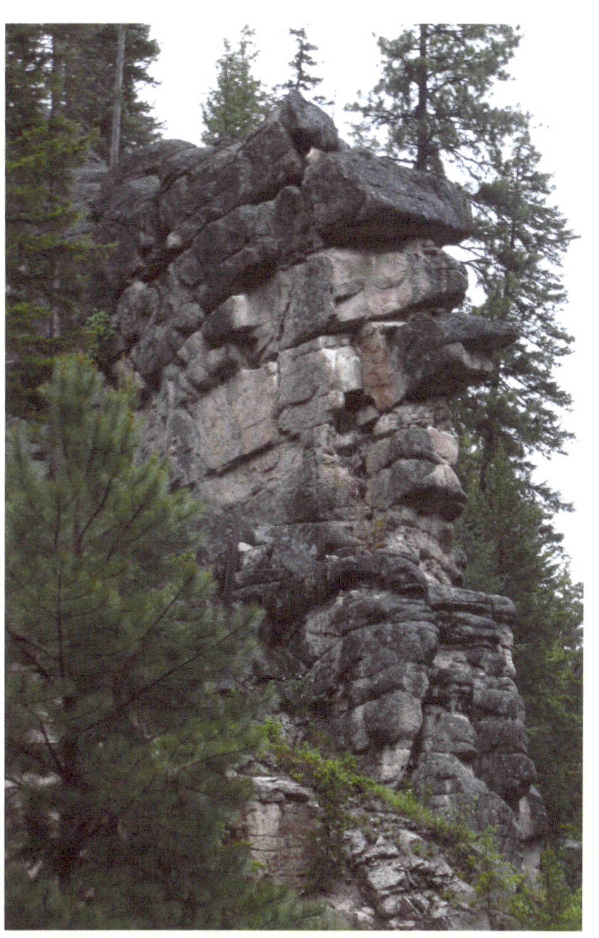

The Lolo Trail was the same trail that had led Lewis and Clark into Nez Perce country.

the group were 20 Flathead Indians. The Flatheads had always been good friends of the Nez Perce. But now they were aiding the whites in hopes of not being ordered onto a reservation themselves.

By July 25 the Nez Perce were near the end of the trail, close to the barricade. Joseph, Looking Class, and White Bird rode up to talk to Captain Rawn.

"Lay down your arms!" demanded the captain.

The Indians refused. "We are going by you without fighting if you will let us," said Chief Joseph, "but we are going by you anyhow."

The Nez Perce promised the whites that they would harm no one in Montana if they were allowed to pass by in peace. At this the Flatheads and volunteers went home. On July 28, all 700 Indians and 2,000 horses hiked past the soldiers into Montana. Captain Rawn's barricade became a joke known as "Fort Fizzle."

In Montana, General Howard was nowhere in sight. And the white people seemed friendly. The Nez Perce jogged their ponies southward, up the wide

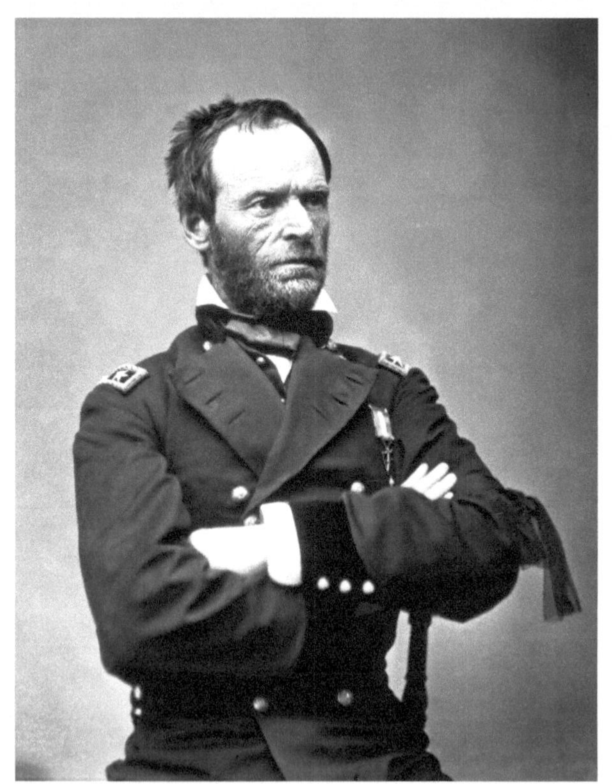

William Tecumseh Sherman, Commanding Ceneral of the Army

Bitterroot Valley. Joseph kept the long line of families moving in an orderly way. Boys drove the herd; women and girls tended the pack animals. No need to hurry. They had left the war behind them in Idaho.

At the little town of Stevensville, the bands stopped to shop, to replace the food and other supplies left behind at the Clearwater fight. They paid the store owners in gold and horses. The chiefs kept a sharp eye on the young men to keep them away from whiskey and out of trouble. Except for a raid on a local ranch, where some men stole food, the chiefs were successful. One store owner called the Nez Perce "...by far the finest looking tribe of Indians I have ever seen..."

Farther along, the bands were joined by a small group of Nez Perce who had been living in the Bitterroot Valley. Among them was a man named Lean Elk, who was half French and half Nez Perce. Fie knew the Montana country well and would be a valued guide on the journey to come.

Some warriors became impatient with Looking Glass's slow pace. Some were having bad dreams. One of these was Shore Crossing, the young man who had started the Salmon River killings in June. Fie rode through the camp crying out, "My brothers, my sisters, I am telling you! In a dream last night I saw myself killed. ... We are all going to die!" And Lone Bird also gave a warning: "My shaking heart tells me trouble and death will overtake us if we make no hurry through this land!"

But Looking Glass was stubborn. "No more fighting!" he insisted. "War is quit."

At the top of the valley, the bands turned eastward and rode to a large, grassy prairie. The whites called this place the Big Hole. To the Nez Perce, it was Place of the Ground Squirrel.

The People had been traveling hard ever since White Bird Canyon. Now by the Big Hole River, in the warm August sun, they could catch up on chores and rest.

Women cut lodge poles from pine trees and set up many buffalo-hide tepees. These were their first proper lodges since leaving their old ones behind at the Clearwater. Men hunted and fished. Children played. On the second night, August 8, a festive parade was held—the first celebration in a long time.

In spite of more warnings from worried people, Chief Looking Glass refused to send out scouts or even post guards at night. The war was over, he reminded everyone.

General Howard *was* still far behind. But Colonel John Gibbon, an officer the Nez Perce did not know, was speeding toward them. Gibbon was Commander of the Seventh Infantry, called "walking soldiers" by the Indians. Gibbon was an experienced Indian fighter. He had a force of about 190 men, some of them volunteers

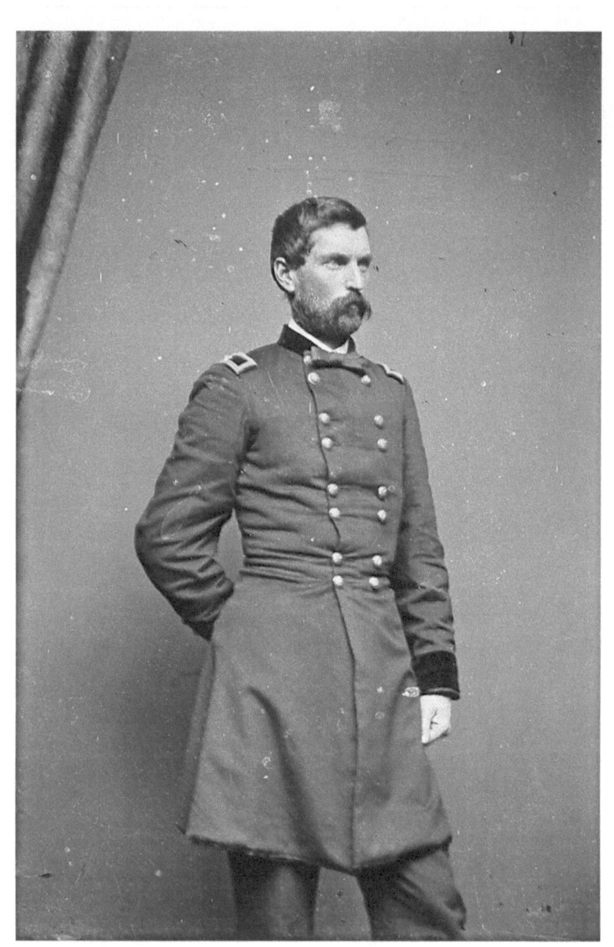

Colonel John Gibbon

to whom he had promised Nez Perce horses.

Gibbon's scouts found the Big Hole village. By the early hours of August 9, his soldiers were hiding in the willows near the Big Hole River. They were ready to attack.

When the first shots rang out, the Indians were sound asleep. Many thought they were dreaming. Bullets started flying, ripping through tepees and into people still wrapped in their buffalo robes. As soldiers charged, warriors searched frantically for their weapons. Joseph, with his baby girl in his arms, dashed out of his lodge to save the horse herd. Women and children huddled on the ground or ran for cover in the willows near the river. Some hid in their tepees, only to be burned alive as soldiers set the lodges on fire.

Warriors who had run out of camp were shooting at the soldiers from every direction. Those still in the camp fought at close range, with guns, war clubs, or just their bare hands. But it looked bad for the Indians. Above the roar White Bird, the oldest chief, could be heard shouting, "Why are we retreating? Since the world was made, brave men fight for their women and children. ... Now is our time. Fight!" And the Nez Perce did fight—with the special fury of men trying to protect the people they love.

Yellow Wolf said, "We now mixed those soldiers badly." By full daylight the warriors were driving the troops out of the village. Gibbon himself was wounded. Fearing a massacre, he called for his men to retreat to a tree-covered hill nearby. There they dug trenches or crouched behind logs. But they were soon surrounded by Nez Perce sharpshooters, whose aim was nearly perfect. Some of the warriors even managed to destroy Gibbon's cannon and capture 2,000 rounds of ammunition. The army's surprise attack had turned into a Nez Perce siege. By battle's end there would be 29 soldiers dead and 40 wounded.

While warriors kept the soldiers pinned down, the rest of the Nez Perce gathered back in the village. Yellow Wolf remembered "Wounded children screaming with pain. Women and

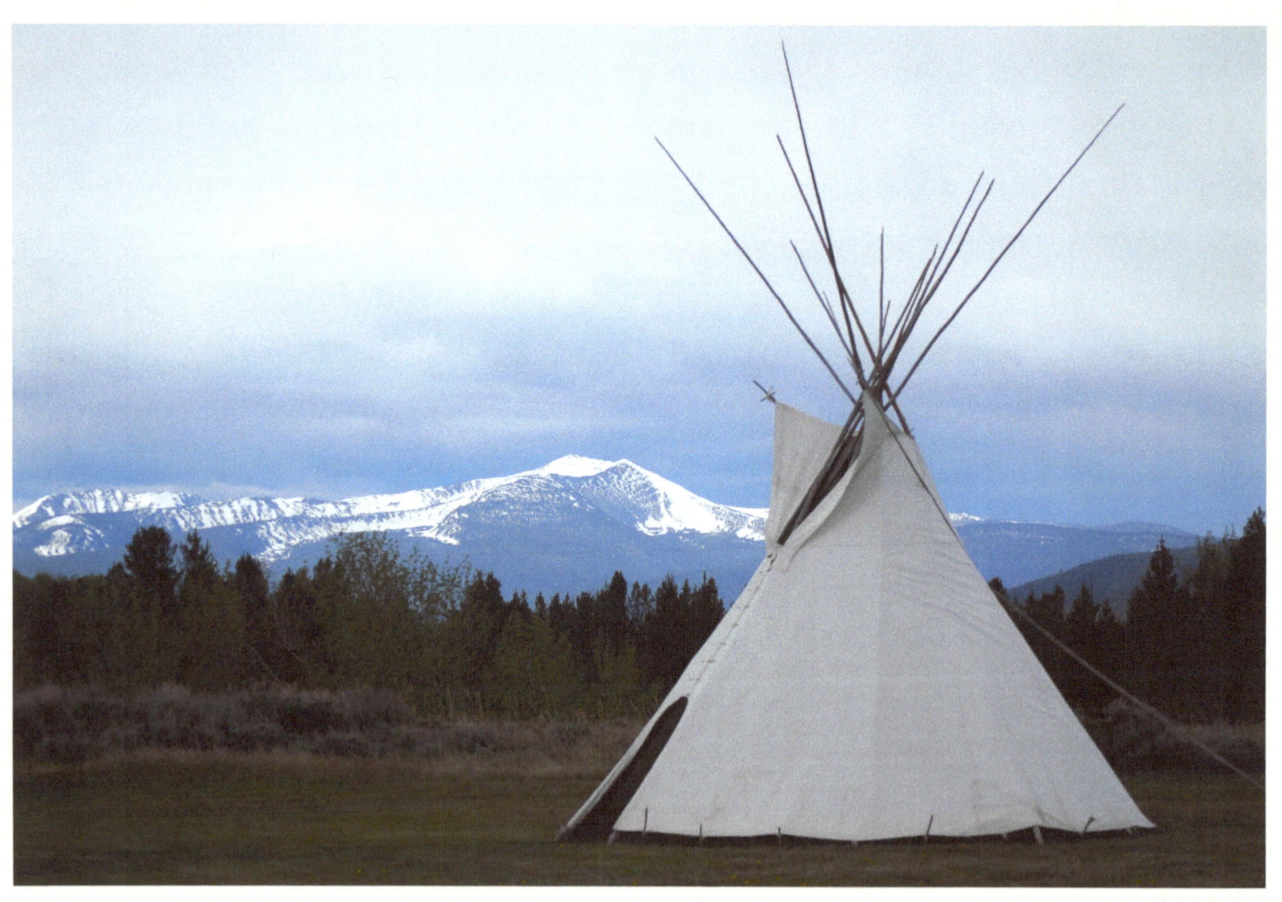

Today Big Hole National Battlefield is located on 655 acres across Montana.

men crying, wailing for their scattered dead! The air was heavy with sorrow." Colonel Gibbon heard the sounds, too: "Few of us will soon forget the wail of mingled grief, rage, and horror... when the Indians...recognized their slaughtered warriors, women, and children."

The Indians quickly buried their dead. By Joseph's count, 50 women and children were killed. Thirty warriors were lost, too, including some of the bravest—Rainbow and Five Wounds, Shore Crossing and Red Moccasin Tops. Joseph's two wives were wounded. Ollokot's wife Fair Land would soon die of her wounds. Almost every family had lost a loved one.

The Battle of the Big Hole was a crushing blow to the Nez Perce. Yet they were not defeated. As Gibbon would later write, "Who would have believed that those Indians would have rallied after such a surprise and made such a fight?"

Chief Joseph had saved the horse herd, so the People were able to escape. He directed them as they took down tepees and packed horses. He helped place the wounded on travois or tie them to their saddles. At noon on that terrible day, he led the sorrowing crowd away from the Big Hole.

Now everyone under stood that they could never leave the war behind.

CHAPTER EIGHT

IN THE WILDS OF YELLOWSTONE

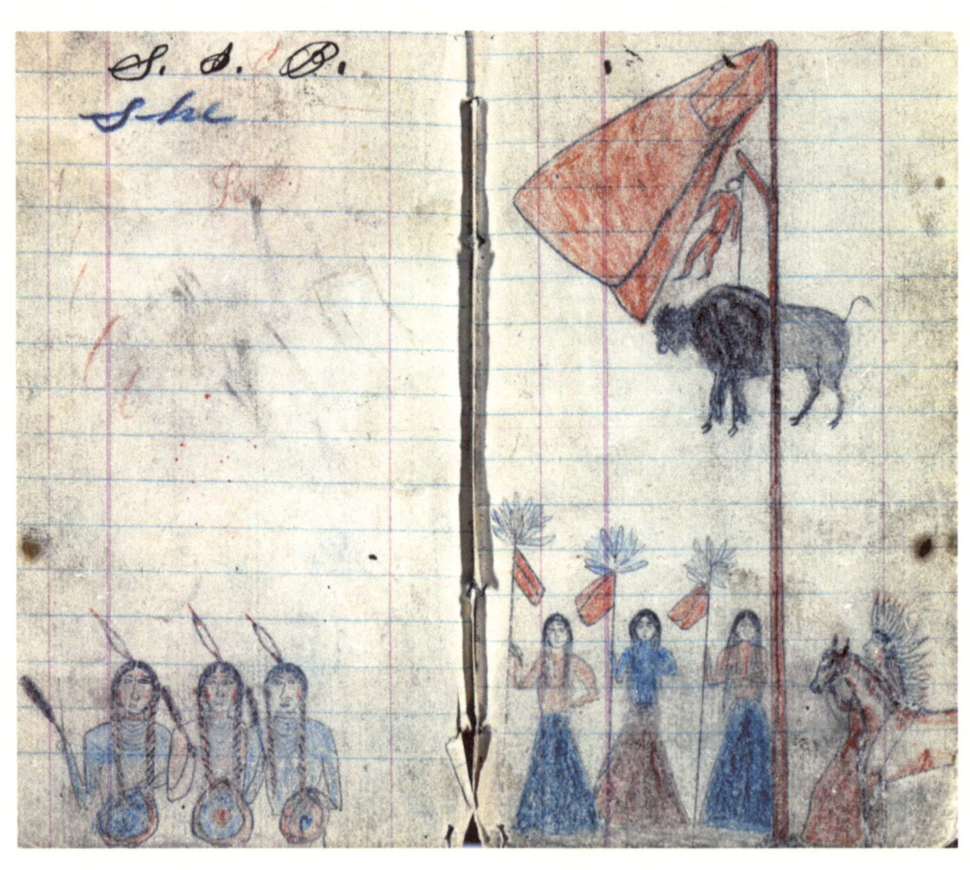

CHIEF JOSEPH'S QUIET strength and courage helped keep the families moving, but many of the wounded died along the trail. Looking Class, who had said the People were safe in Montana, was no longer in charge. The new war leader was Lean Elk. He and Joseph set a fast pace. Their route took them south, along the edge of the Bitterroot Mountains. They stayed as far from white settlements as possible.

The Big Hole had changed everything. Now the Nez Perce saw all whites as enemies. Some who had attacked their camp were the same men they had traded with in the Bitterroot Valley. In just the first week after the battle, enraged warriors raided ranches, looted freight wagons, stole hundreds of horses, and killed ten white men.

Meanwhile General Howard had arrived at the battle scene. After helping Gibbon's wounded, he and his men marched off again after the Indians. He learned from two treaty Nez Perce that the hostiles were headed to buffalo country. Howard took a shortcut and caught up. By August 19 he was camped on a prairie called Camas Meadows, only one day behind the Indians.

Nez Perce scouts saw the soldiers coming and warned the tribe. Now the chiefs and warriors planned a daring raid. They would sneak into Howard's camp and steal all his horses—maybe put a stop to the general's endless pursuit.

Twenty-eight warriors smoked the pipe together. They called on their wyakin for help. Before dawn on August 20, they rode quietly to the edge of the well-guarded soldier camp. Some of the Indians crept among the sleeping men and started untying horses. Suddenly a nervous warrior fired his gun. Startled soldiers began shooting into the darkness. Waving blankets, whooping, and hollering, the Indians stampeded all the loose animals out of camp.

When daylight broke, the raiders were disappointed to see that they had stolen mules instead of horses! At least Howard would have no way to carry his supplies. Almost his whole train of pack mules was gone.

The cavalry galloped over the sagebrush after the warriors, only to find them lying in wait in the hills beyond the camp. In a sharp fight, the Indians surrounded Howard's men and killed three. As Howard himself hurried to the scene, the warriors rode off to join the families on the trail. "We had no ordinary Indians to deal with," noted one soldier.

General Howard's men were "sick and tired" of chasing Indians all over the West. They were cold and ragged, too. Some had no shoes. Howard allowed the troops a short rest. While his men relaxed, he traveled to Virginia City, Montana, to buy badly needed supplies. New pack mules were high on the shopping list.

The general, too, had had enough. He sent a telegram to General Sherman, describing his tired men and tired animals. "I cannot push it much further," Howard wrote.

Sherman replied, "...that force of yours should pursue the Nez Perces to the death. ... If you are tired, give the command to some young, energetic officer..."

Ashamed to be thought a quitter, Howard returned to his men with fresh determination to catch the Indians. He knew that their path to the buffalo plains would take them through the Yellowstone region in Wyoming.

Yellowstone was a strange place of hot springs, geysers, and colorful, boiling mudpots. It was established

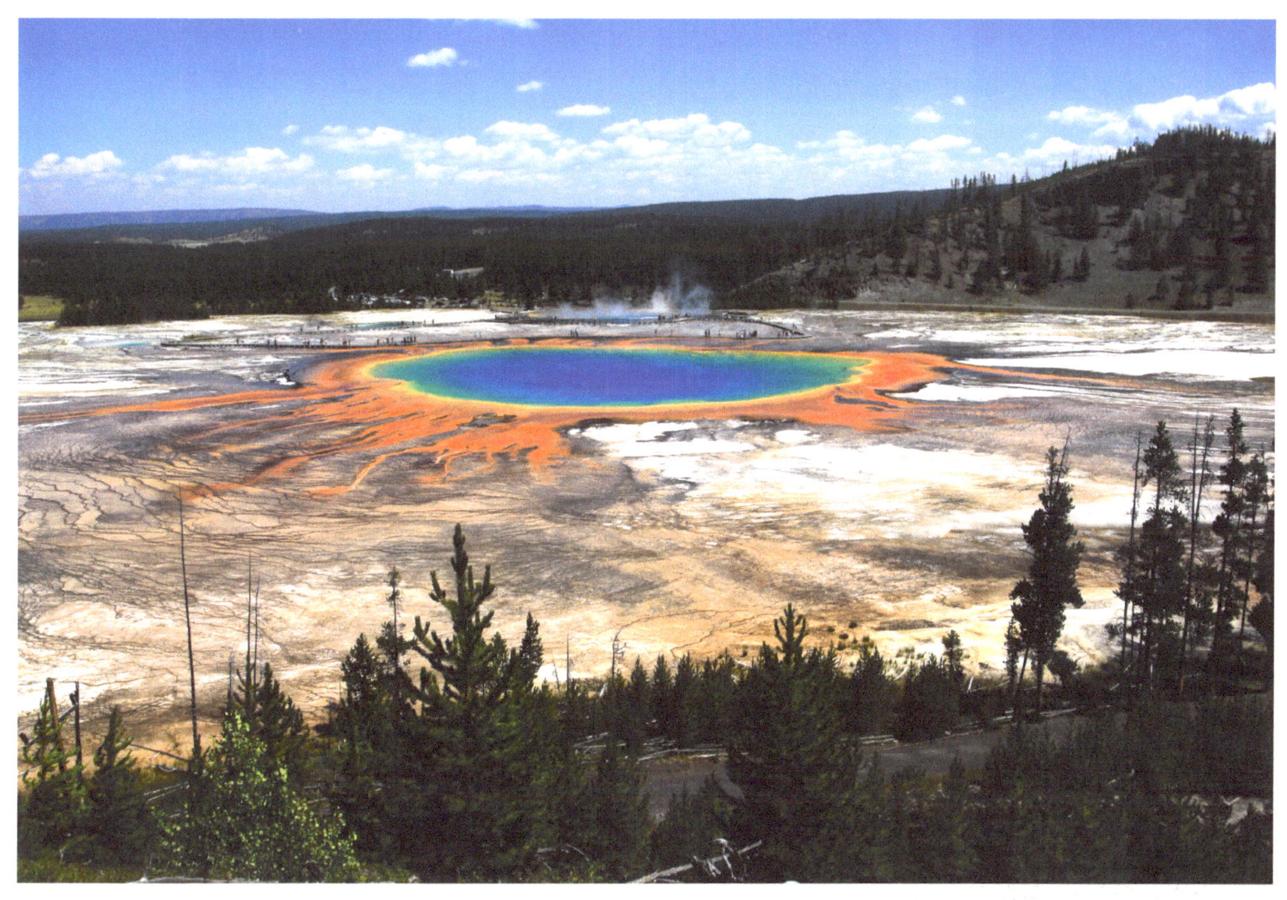

Hot springs at Yellowstone National Park are created by heat from molten rock deep inside the earth. It comes up and penetrates rock and water until the hot water escapes at the ground's surface.

as America's first national park in 1872. In 1877 it was still a mysterious wilderness. The weary Nez Perce entered the park on August 23. Soon their scouting parties found that they were not alone.

Yellow Wolfs party grabbed a miner named John Shively and held him until he escaped several days later. Shively served as a guide to the Indians because for a short time, Lean Elk was unsure of his route.

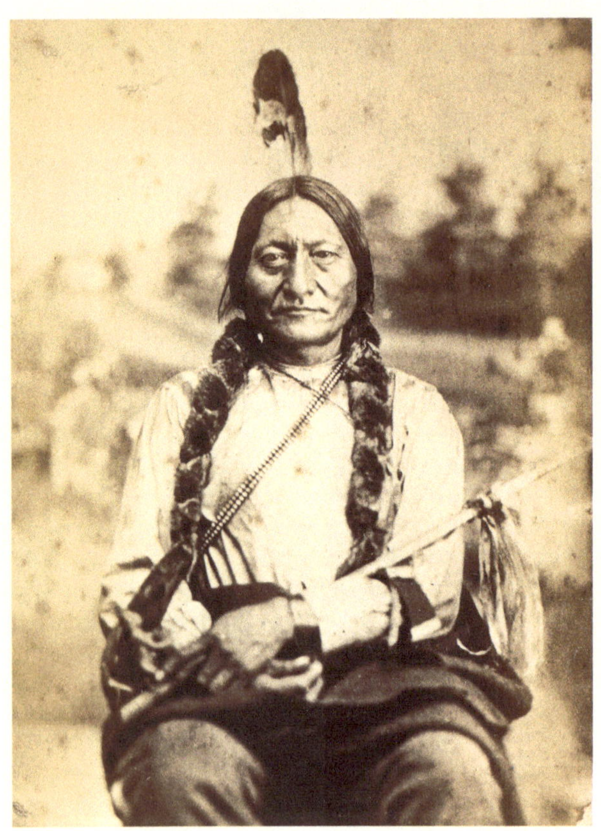

The great Sioux leader, Sitting Bull, fought hard to keep his homeland in the buffalo country of the Great Plains. Facing starvation in Canada, he finally surrendered to the Americans in 1881.

Then Yellow Wolf's scouts discovered a group of Montana tourists and took them captive. On the trail another scouting party attacked the whites. Two were shot and wounded, but most escaped. The remaining captives, Emma Cowan and her sister and brother, were placed under the protection of the chiefs. Emma spent a long night at Chief Joseph's campfire. Later she described how Joseph sat silent, lost in thought: "Grave and dignified, he looked a chief." The next day the three tourists were given horses and set free. Worried about their safety. Lean Elk told them to go quickly.

In the days that followed, Nez Perce scouts killed two white men and spread terror through the park. The warriors wanted revenge for the Big Hole. And to them, all whites were spies for the army. Across America, newspapers were bursting with sensational news from Yellowstone. Many of the stories featured Chief Joseph, the "military genius."

The Nez Perce climbed up into the rugged Absaroka Mountains on the eastern border of the park. They were still headed to the buffalo country of the Crow Indians. But now they planned only to pass through it. The chiefs had

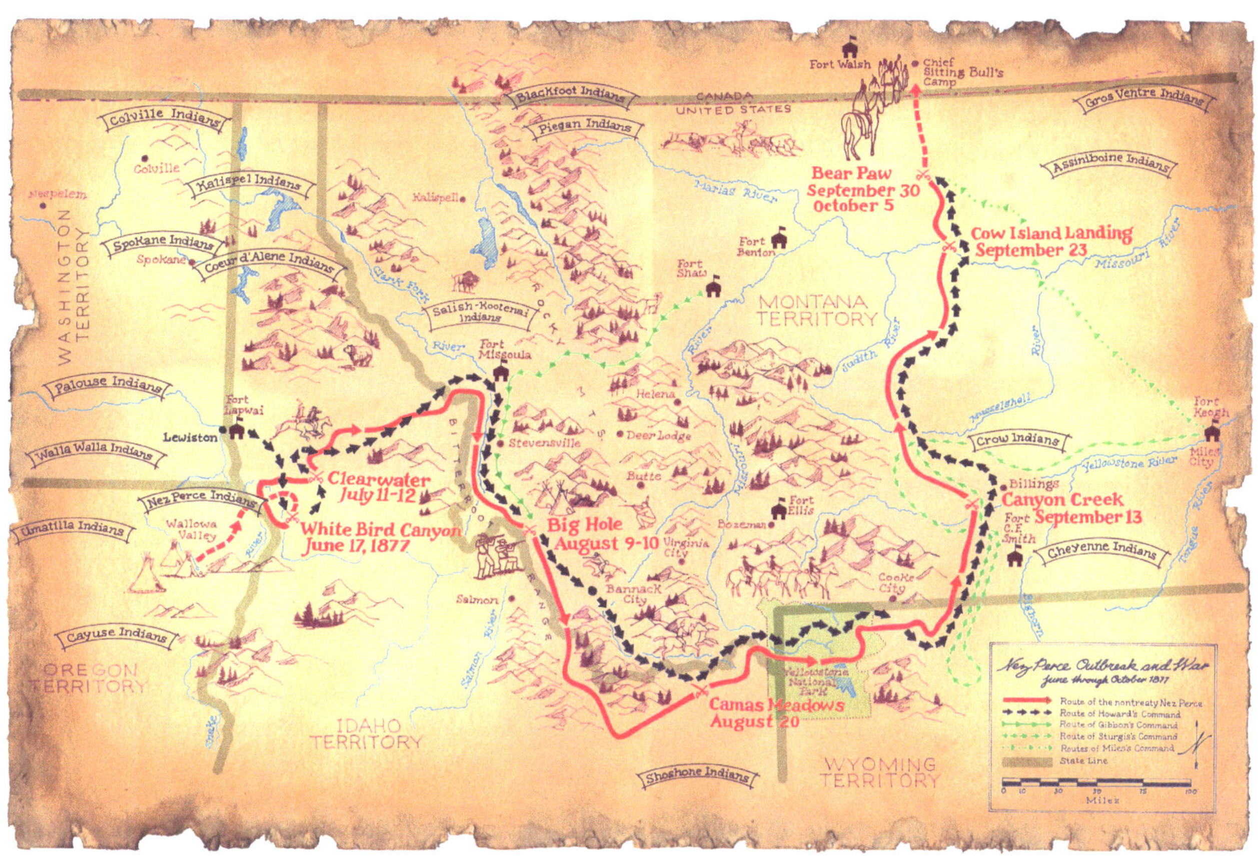

The Nez Perce route is 1,170 miles long, starting at Wallowa Lake and stretching to Bear Paw Battleground.

decided on a new destination.

Just the year before, in 1876, the Sioux and Cheyenne Indians had defeated the United States Army at the Battle of the Little Bighorn. "Custer's Last Stand," it was often called. Even so, in the months after the battle, these tribes had been herded onto reservations. Only the famous Sioux leader Sitting Bull and his band were still living free. They had escaped to Canada. After their own fight at the Big Hole, the Nez Perce chiefs realized that Canada was the only place where they might find peace and freedom, too.

While the families struggled through the Absarokas, the army was busy setting a trap. General Sherman placed troops at every Yellowstone exit. Wherever the Indians came down from the mountains to leave the park, soldiers would be there to block their escape. And with Howard on the trail behind them, the tribe would be caught between two armies. It was a foolproof plan.

But once again the Nez Perce outsmarted the army. They left Yellowstone by a path so difficult that it was considered impossible to travel. By the time Howard followed them out of the mountains, the families were about 50 miles ahead of him on the Montana prairie.

CHAPTER NINE

I WILL FIGHT NO MORE FOREVER

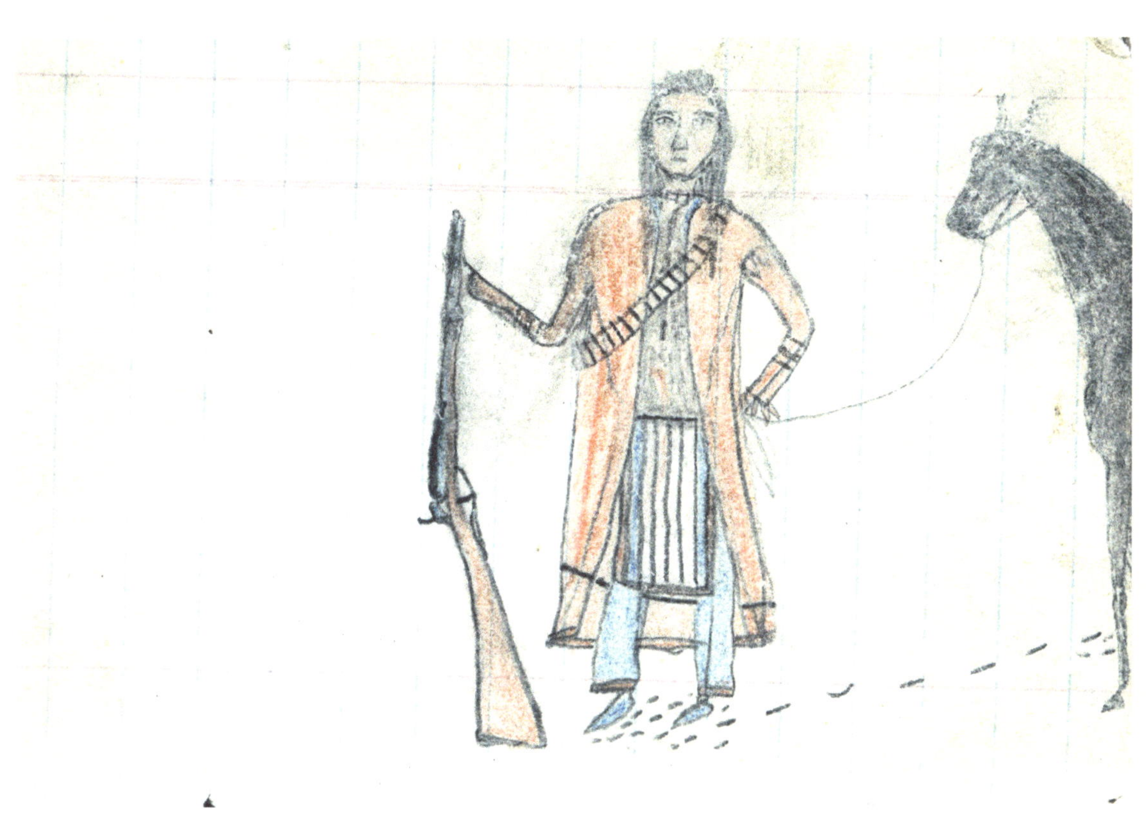

ONLY 300 MILES to go. There were no more mountains to climb—just the rolling plains of buffalo country ahead. With their minds fixed on Canada, the Nez Perce rode steadily north.

But now another large body of cavalry, under Colonel Samuel Sturgis, was racing after them. On September 13, Sturgis caught up with the Indians at Canyon Creek, a dry creek bed with high canyon walls. The warriors easily held off Sturgis's men while the families fled to the safety of the canyon. Sturgis gave up and camped that night near Canyon Creek. Soon Howard joined him there. Once again the Nez Perce warriors had left the army in the dust.

The bands were in Crow country now. Yet they had received no help from the tribe that Looking Glass called "my brothers." Instead, the Crows were scouting for Colonel Sturgis—against their old friends. After the fight at Canyon Creek, a large party of Crows attacked the Nez Perce, stealing horses and killing three men. When Yellow Wolf saw them coming, he said, "My heart was just like fire." The warriors fought off these new enemies, too. But they fought bitterly; these had once been their friends.

Still the People kept going. On September 23 they splashed their horses across the great Missouri River at a place called Cow Island. Here the army kept a storage depot, loaded with food and supplies. It was guarded by only a handful of soldiers. When the officer in charge refused to sell food to the hungry Indians, they decided to take it. Covered by the warriors' gunfire, the families seized what they needed—flour, bacon, sugar, beans, even pots and pans. After setting the depot ablaze, the Nez Perce rode off again.

After more than three months

of hard and heartbreaking travel, they were exhausted. Their horses' feet were sore. And now the winds of autumn were blowing across the plains, blowing cold during the long marches. Looking Glass wanted to slow down, so he was chosen to lead again. But Lean Elk, who had brought the bands so far, still favored speed. "All right. Looking Glass, you can lead," he said, "...but I think we will be caught and killed."

On September 29 the Nez Perce camped near the Bear Paw Mountains. Canada was just 40 miles away. The Indians had no more tepees, only a few canvas shelters. These they set up in the hollows along a little stream called Snake Creek. Bluffs at the edges of the camp gave some protection from the biting wind. Men killed buffalo on the prairie, and women cooked the meat over fires fueled by buffalo "chips," or manure. The People rested because they knew that the soldiers were days behind.

They were wrong. General Howard had asked for help from Colonel

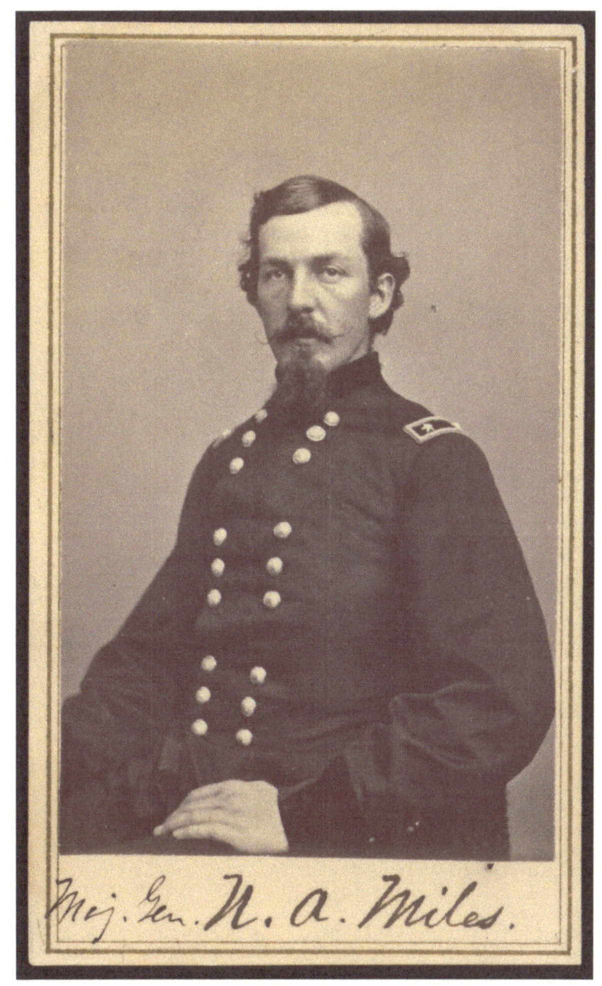

Colonel Nelson A. Miles

Nelson Miles, stationed at Fort Keogh in eastern Montana. Miles had played a key role in the defeat of the Sioux and Cheyenne after the Battle of the Little Bighorn. He was eager to conquer the Nez Perce, too. Quickly he organized a command of about 400 soldiers, including a group of pro-white Sioux and Cheyenne scouts. Then he marched at top speed across Montana. Miles hoped to cut off the hostiles before they reached Canada.

As the Nez Perce rested at the Bear Paw, Colonel Miles and his soldiers were drawing very near.

At breakfast time on September 30, a Nez Perce scout appeared on a bluff, madly waving a blanket in the air. This was the signal that meant "Enemies right on us! Soon the attack!" Warriors grabbed their guns. Women screamed for their children. "Horses! Horses! Save the horses!" shouted Joseph, as he and others ran to the herd.

Then came a pounding noise like a buffalo stampede. Hoofbeats shook the ground as hundreds of Miles's cavalrymen charged the camp. Many Indians were caught amid their frightened ponies. They jumped on the first animal they could catch and escaped toward the north. Joseph put his 12-year-old daughter Kapkap Ponmi on a horse. He told her to run for her life. Then he dashed back to camp to fight, bullets whizzing all around him.

Warriors and soldiers were shooting at close range now. The Indians, hidden behind rocks and slopes in the land, beat back the first terrifying charge. They killed or wounded 53 soldiers. Miles ordered a second charge. Then a third. Against all odds the warriors drove back each one. "I never went up against anything like the Nez Perce in all my life," said one soldier. Miles was shocked. Since he couldn't beat the enemy in battle, he decided to starve them out by holding a siege.

That night it snowed. Warriors dug rifle pits, while women dug shelters and tunnels in the earth for their families. Children cried. It was freezing, and there was little food. Twenty-two people were dead, including the beloved leaders Lean Elk, Toohoolhoolzote, and Ollokot. They had been "swept away as leaves before the storm," said Yellow Wolf.

The people were trapped now because the soldiers had succeeded in capturing most of the horses. Even so, six men slipped away and rode toward Sitting Bull's camp. Only the fighting Sioux could help them now.

The siege continued the next day. Guns blazed on both sides. In later years Yellow Wolf remembered, "I felt the end coming. All for which we had suffered lost!" And his thoughts turned to the Wallowa Valley, so far away. But his wyakin, the "Wolf-Power," had made him strong. He resolved to fight to the death.

Miles sent out the white flag of truce and asked to talk to Chief Joseph. Bringing with him a man who spoke English, Joseph rode to a spot halfway between the two camps to meet the Colonel. Here Miles made a promise: If the Indians surrendered, they would spend the winter at Fort Keogh. And in the spring, they would go to the Nez Perce reservation at Lapwai, Idaho, to live.

But the talks broke down. Then, in spite of the white flag. Miles took Joseph prisoner. In return the Nez Perce captured an army officer. This ruined Miles's plan to hold Joseph until the Indians surrendered. The next day the two hostages were exchanged, and the fighting resumed.

Days and nights passed slowly. It was bitter cold. Many Indians, huddling in their underground shelters, were near freezing to death. On October 4, the fifth day of the siege. General Howard arrived. Now the Nez Perce feared another cavalry charge.

The next day Howard sent two treaty Nez Perce to the Indian camp with a message. The army wanted no more war, Howard said. And like Miles, he promised that if the bands surrendered, they could return to Idaho in the spring. They would get their horses back, too.

Joseph, Looking Class, and White Bird held a last desperate council. Both White Bird and Looking Glass said they would never surrender. They did not trust white men's promises. "I have my experiences with a man of two faces and two tongues," said Looking Glass. "If you surrender, you will be sorry; and in your sorrow you will feel rather to be dead..."

But Joseph was the protector of the families. He wanted to save the lives of the old, the wounded, the little children. "For myself I do not care," he answered. "It is for them I am going to surrender."

In the Nez Perce tradition, each person is free to go his own way, so the chiefs accepted Joseph's decision. Soon after the council. Looking Glass was killed by a bullet from the soldier camp. Now Joseph and White Bird were the only chiefs left.

In the cold, gray afternoon of October 5, 1877, Joseph prepared to do the hardest thing he had ever done. He mounted his horse, placed his rifle across his saddle, and rode up to meet the enemy. Five trusted warriors walked beside his horse, talking to their chief the whole way.

Chief Joseph handed Colonel Miles his rifle, then gave a surrender speech that told the tragedy of his people:

Tell General Howard I know his heart. What he told me before I have in my heart. I am tired of fighting. Our chiefs are killed. Looking Glass is dead. Toohoolhoolzote is dead. The old men are all dead. It is the young men who say yes or no. He [Ollokot] who led on the young men is dead. It is cold and we have no blankets. The little children are freezing to

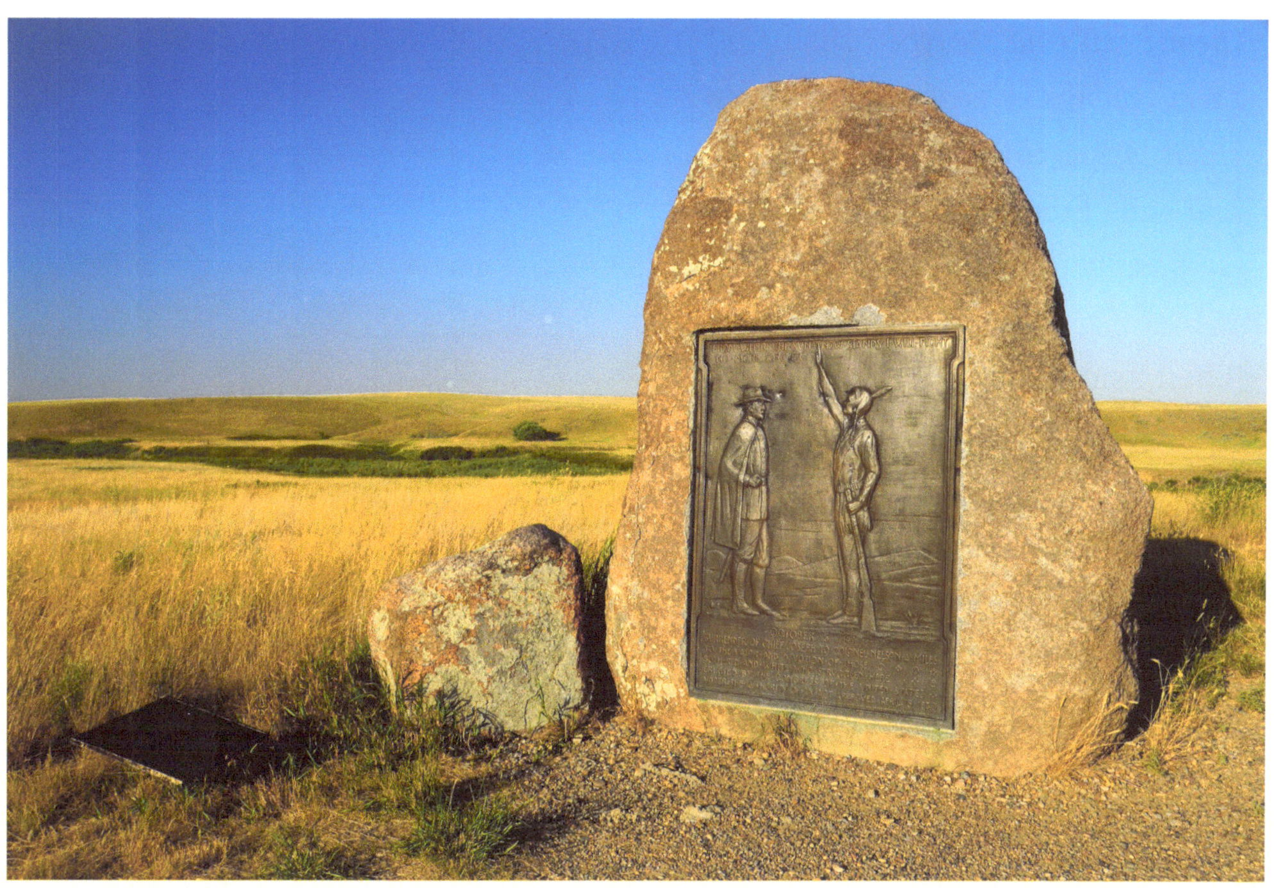

Today people can visit the Bear Paw Memorial, where Chief Joseph surrendered only 40 miles from the Canadian border. This marks the end of the Nez Perce's trail.

death. My people, some of them, have run away to the hills and have no blankets, no food; no one knows where they are—perhaps freezing to death. I want to have time to look for my children and see how many of them I can find. Maybe I shall find them among the dead. Hear me, my chiefs, I am tired; my heart is sick and sad. From where the sun now stands, I will fight no more forever.

Then, slowly, up from the Indian camp came all the People—more than 400—who chose to surrender with Chief Joseph. Wounded, cold, and starving, they accepted blankets and food from the soldiers. The heroic Nez Perce fight for freedom was over.

Nelson Miles called it "...the most fierce of any Indian engagement I have ever been in." It was also the last great Indian War in the settling of the American West. About 200 warriors had battled close to 1,400 soldiers for four months over a distance of 1,700 miles. Yet the Indians had never wanted war. They had only wanted to keep their home.

CHAPTER TEN

ONE SKY ABOVE US

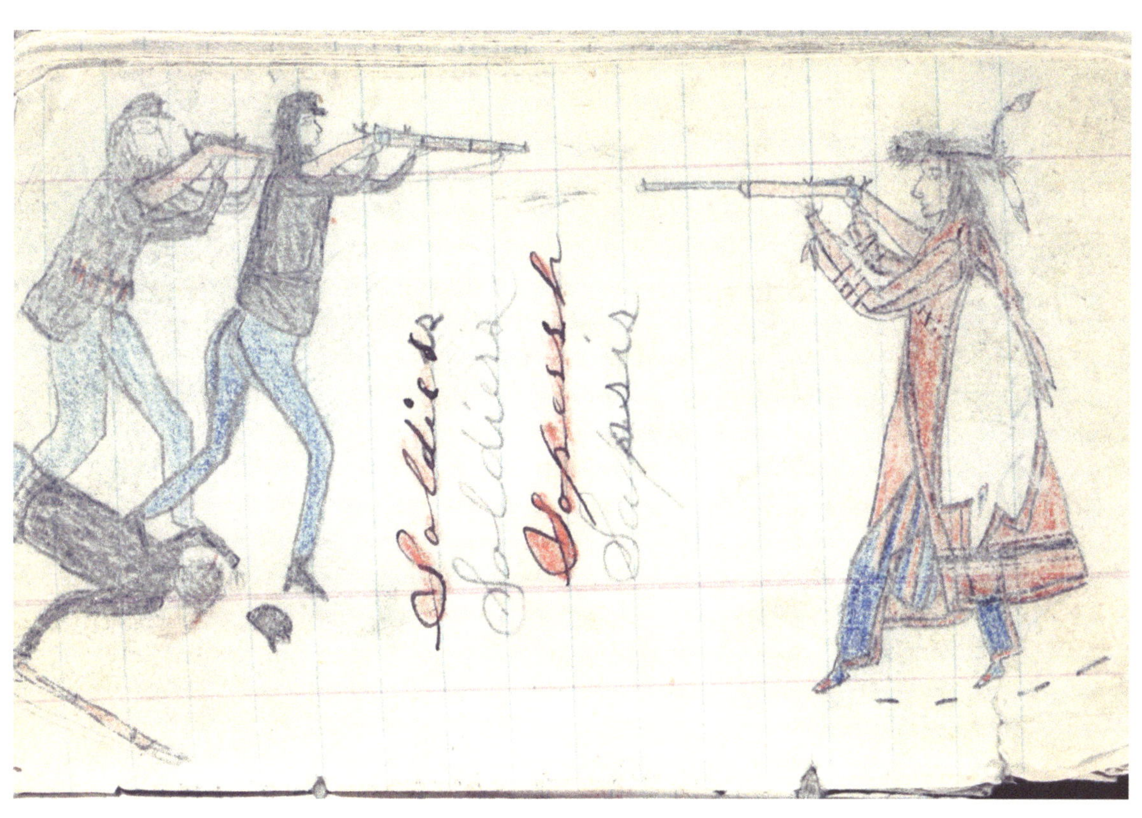

SOME CHOSE NOT to surrender. That night, after Joseph handed over his rifle, White Bird and about 50 others fled silently on foot toward Canada. Ollokot's wife, now a widow, was part of this group. "It was lonesome, the leaving..." she said. "I felt I was leaving all that I had, but I did not cry." Yellow Wolf, probably the last to go, escaped alone into the black night.

From the first to the last day of the Bear Paw fight, more than 200 Nez Perce ran toward Sitting Bull's camp. Some were killed along the way. Some were taken prisoner by soldiers. But those who made it to Canada were welcomed by the Sioux, their old enemies. They were treated with great kindness. The earliest group of warriors who had come to Sitting Bull for help had failed to clearly explain the location of the battle. By the time the Sioux chief sent out a war party, the fight was over. There was nothing to do but bury the dead.

Back in Montana Chief Joseph and his followers faced an ordeal harder than fighting. They were now prisoners of war. While General Howard's men returned to their army posts. Miles led his long line of captives back across Montana to Fort Keogh. There he expected the Indians to spend the winter before joining the rest of their tribe at Lapwai.

But at Fort Keogh, Miles learned that General Sherman had other ideas. According to Sherman the Nez Perce "should never again be allowed to return to Oregon or Lapwai." Citizens in the Northwest wanted revenge for the Salmon River killings, Sherman noted. Besides, he argued, the hostiles should be severely punished for daring to fight. Sherman wanted to send them to Indian Territory, a huge area in present-day Oklahoma that had been set aside for displaced tribes.

General Howard soon sided with Sherman. But Miles was anxious to keep his word to Joseph. He spoke out in favor of returning the Nez Perce to the Northwest. It did no good.

Miles was ordered to move the captives to Fort Lincoln, near Bismarck, North Dakota. Another long trip—hundreds of miles—for the worried Indians. The strong ones rode overland with Miles. The wounded and weak traveled by boat down the icy Missouri River.

Both Miles and the Indians were greeted in Bismarck by a brass band. Townspeople gave food to the hungry Nez Perce. A dinner was even held in Chief Joseph's honor. All the publicity during the war, as well as his moving surrender speech, had made the chief a celebrity.

But in North Dakota, Joseph learned that his people were to be sent to Indian Territory. They would be exiled from their own land, maybe forever. Another broken promise. "When will those white chiefs begin to tell the truth?" he asked. In Bismarck, Colonel Miles said goodbye to Joseph. In the coming years, he would try to help the Nez Perce in their effort to get home.

In late November the prisoners traveled by train to Fort Leavenworth, Kansas. There they had to camp on swampy ground. Many of them contracted malaria, a disease carried by the mosquitoes that swarmed around them. The army gave no medicine to the Indians. At least 21 people died. "I cannot tell you how much my heart suffered for my people while at Leavenworth," said Joseph. "The Great Spirit Chief who rules above seemed to be looking some other way, and did not see what was being done to my people."

At Leavenworth control of the

Nez Perce was moved from the War Department back to the Indian Bureau. Like General Sherman, officials in the Bureau ignored the promise that Miles and Howard had made. So in July 1878, the families moved again. Their new "home" was the Quapaw reservation, in Indian Territory.

When they arrived at Quapaw, they found that no preparations had been made. There was no housing or medical care. And many people were still suffering from malaria. By October 1878, 47 more Nez Perce had died, including almost all the newborn babies.

More exiles joined Chief Joseph's people. Yellow Wolf and others had grown homesick in Canada and had made their way back to Lapwai. Some of them, such as Joseph's daughter Kapkap Ponmi, were allowed to stay in Idaho. But Yellow Wolf and other warriors in his group were sent to Indian Territory. At Quapaw, in the smothering heat, the Indians dreamed of the snowy mountains and cold waters of home. They called Indian Territory "the Hot Place."

They were lost in a nightmare of despair and death. Another move within the Hot Place, this time to the Ponca reservation, made little difference. One by one the children were still dying. One of these was Joseph's baby girl, born at the Split Rocks camp at the beginning of the war.

Even in the earliest days of exile, Joseph began fighting to make the government honor the Bear Paw promise."! believed General Miles, or I never would have surrendered," he said. He sent a petition to Washington, D.C. He spoke to everyone who visited Indian Territory—reporters, men from the Indian Bureau, members of Congress, and private citizens. Finally he received permission to meet with President Rutherford B. Hayes.

Joseph went to Washington, D.C., in January 1879, with his friend Yellow Bull. Ad Chapman went along as their interpreter. In addition to seeing the President, Joseph gave a speech to a large audience of politicians and other influential people. In his striped blanket coat and moccasins, he stood before a sea of strange faces and told the whole story of his people. For two hours he spoke straight from his heart.

He spoke of Lewis and Clark, of missionaries and miners, of treaties—and how the Nez Perce were robbed of their country. Of the Wallowa Valley, Joseph said, "If we ever owned the land we own it still, for we never sold it."

He described his struggle to avoid war, and how "deeply grieved" he was when it started. And he talked about each battle, from the first one at White Bird Canyon to the last at the Bear Paw Mountains.

And all the broken promises! "I cannot understand," said Joseph, "how the Government sends a man out to fight us, as it did General Miles, and then breaks his word." Not even the Indians' horses had been returned, Joseph said.

He wanted action, not just words: "Good words will not get my people a home..."

Then he talked about his love of freedom. "You might as well expect the rivers to run backward as that any man who was born a free man should be contented when penned up. ... Let me be a free man..."

Finally Chief Joseph spoke about the equality of all people. "All men were made by the same Great Spirit Chief. They are all brothers. ... Whenever the white man treats the Indian as they treat each other, then we will have

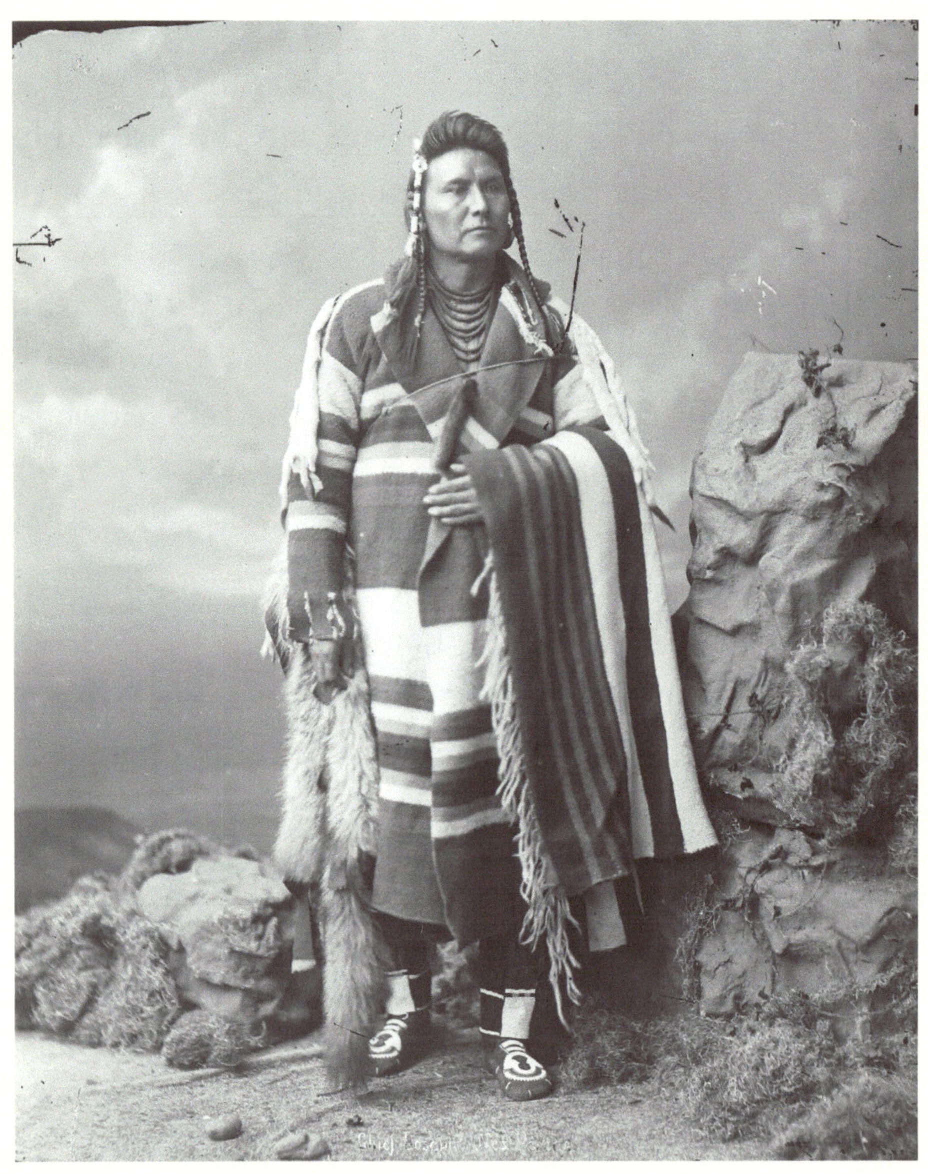

Chief Joseph's speech is one of the most memorable in American history. In it he spoke of freedom and equality for all people. He became the symbol of his people's struggle, and his remarkable life is still an inspiration today.

no more wars. We shall all be alike—brothers of one father and one mother, with one sky above us and one country around us, and one government for all. Then the Great Spirit Chief who rules above will smile upon this land…"

No one who heard the famous chief that day ever forgot his words.

Afterward Joseph and Yellow Bull had to return to the Hot Place. But the movement to help the Nez Perce was growing stronger. Nelson Miles, now a general, was still trying. And hundreds of people wrote letters and signed petitions.

In 1883 a small group of widows and children was allowed to return to Lapwai. Worn out with suffering, they held their long-lost tribesmen and wept.

At last the Indian Bureau freed all the Nez Perce from exile. On May 22, 1885, Joseph and his remaining followers boarded a train for the long ride back to the Northwest. Out of the more than 400 people sent to Indian Territory, only 268 were left to take that ride. Almost half had died in exile.

Idaho citizens were furious about the return of Chief Joseph. They still blamed him for the Nez Perce War. A sheriff waited to arrest him for the murders of white settlers. Many treaty Nez Perce at Lapwai considered him a troublemaker, too. So the Indian Bureau sent Joseph to live on the Colville reservation in Washington. Others on the train may have had a choice between Lapwai and Colville. Yellow Wolf was asked, "Where [do] you want to go? Lapwai and be Christian, or Colville and just be yourself?" A Dreamer and a warrior, he chose Colville.

Joseph and his loyal followers tried to rebuild their lives on the Washington reservation. They learned to grow some crops, but mostly they lived in the old way—hunting, gathering plants, raising horses. Although the government built a few cheap houses for the Indians, Joseph always preferred his tepee. And he never stopped trying to get back to Oregon.

In 1899 he saw the Wallowa Valley again, for the first time in 22 years. Small towns, farms, and ranches now dotted the meadows where Nez Perce horses had galloped and grazed. Joseph asked the settlers to sell him a small piece of land for his people. But they refused. On a later visit, Joseph stood by his father's grave and wept. Again his request to buy land was turned down. Still he did not give up. "I love that land more than all the rest of the world."

But his body was tired and weighed down with sorrow. On September 21, 1904, as he sat in front of his tepee fire, dreaming perhaps of his beautiful valley of winding waters, Chief Joseph suddenly died. He was 64 years old.

He had not been able to protect his father's grave, but he had kept his promise in other ways. He had guided the families, held them together during their fight for freedom and their long years of exile. He had seen to it that his followers were returned to the Northwest. And if he had not been able to bring them all the way home, he had done something else that would never be forgotten. Chief Joseph had spoken for his people.

SOURCES FOR QUOTATIONS

Beal, Merrill D. *"I Will Fight No More Forever": Chief Joseph and the Nez Perce War.* New York: Ballantine Books, 1971.

Chief Joseph. *"An Indian's Views of Indian Affairs."* North American Review (April 1879).

Gulick, Bill. *Chief Joseph Country: Land of the Nez Perce.* Caldwell, Idaho: The Caxton Printers, Ltd., 1994.

Hampton, Bruce. *Children of Grace: The Nez Perce War of 1877.* Lincoln and London: University of Nebraska Press, 2002.

Josephy, Alvin M., Jr. *The Nez Perce Indians and the Opening of the Northwest.* New Haven and London: Yale University Press, 1965.

Lavender, David. *Let Me Be Free: The Nez Perce Tragedy.* New York: HarperCollins Publishers, 1992.

McWhorter, Lucullus Virgil. *Hear Me, My Chiefs!* Caldwell, Idaho: The Caxton Printers, Ltd., 1992.

McWhorter, Lucullus Virgil. *Yellow Wolf, His Own Story.* Caldwell, Idaho; Caxton Press, 2000.

Moulton, Candy. *Chief Joseph, Guardian of the People*. New York: Forge, 2005.

Utley, Robert M. *The Indian Frontier of the American West 1846-1890*. Albuquerque: University of New Mexico Press, 1984.

Wilfong, Cheryl. *Following the Nez Perce Trail*. Corvallis, Oregon: Oregon State University Press, 1990.

ABOUT THE AUTHOR

Former Western Writers of America president, Nancy Plain is an award-winning author of children's and young adult nonfiction. Recognition for her work includes four Spur Awards for Best Western Juvenile Nonfiction, the YALSA Excellence in Nonfiction Finalist Award, two Nebraska Book Awards, the National Outdoor Book Award, the Will Rogers Gold Medallion, and more. Her biography of John James Audubon, This Strange Wilderness, earned starred reviews from Booklist and Kirkus, was named a Booklist "Editors' Choice", cited by Kirkus as one of "Nine Teen Titles That Adults Shouldn't Miss", and chosen to represent the state of Nebraska at the 2017 National Book Festival, in Washington, D.C.

Nancy lives in New Jersey with her husband Alan. When not exploring the West, she can often be found at home, reading and writing its thrilling history, for she believes young readers love true stories, too.

www.ingramcontent.com/pod-product-compliance
Lightning Source LLC
LaVergne TN
LVHW070217110826
845147LV00003B/591

* 9 7 8 1 9 5 3 9 4 4 9 6 2 *